Horizons Writing

Stella Sands

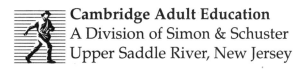

Cambridge Adult Education
A Division of Simon & Schuster
Upper Saddle River, New Jersey

Executive Editor: Mark Moscowitz
Project Editors: Robert McIlwaine, Bernice Golden, Keisha Carter, Laura Baselice, Lynn Kloss
Writer: Stella Sands
Series Editor: Roberta Mantus
Consultants/Reviewers: Marjorie Jacobs, Cecily Kramer Bodnar
Production Manager: Penny Gibson
Production Editor: Nicole Cypher
Marketing Manager: Will Jarred
Interior Electronic Design: Flanagan's Publishing Services, Inc.
Illustrator: Accurate Art, Inc.
Photo Research: Jenifer Hixson
Electronic Page Production: Flanagan's Publishing Services, Inc.
Cover Design: Armando Baéz

Photo Credits: p.3: Alexander Lowry/Photo Researchers; p.6: Rafael Macia/Photo Researchers; p.12: Gillian and Scott Aldrich; p.15: The Granger Collection; p.18: Radi Nabulsi; p.21: Eunice Harris, The Picture Cube; p.23: Laima Druskis/Photo Researchers; p.26: Spencer Grant/Photo Researchers; p.29: Michael Siluk, Picture Cube; p.32: M.E. Warren Photo Researchers; p.35: Library of Congress; p.39: New York Historical Society; p.42: Barbara Rios/Photo Researchers; p.45: Scott and Gillian Aldrich; p.50: UPI/Bettmann; p.53: Mark D. Philips/Photo Researchers; p.54: Scott and Gillian Aldrich; p.57: Barbara Rios/Photo Researchers; p.61: Scott and Gillian Aldrich; p.64: Freda Leinwand; p.73: Wide World Photos; p.74: The Bettmann Archive; p.81: Scott and Gillian Aldrich; p.89: Photo Researchers; p.91: Bettye Land/Photo Researchers; p.93: Courtesy of Knopf. Photo ©Kate Kunz; p.95: UPI/Bettmann; p.97: Jeff Greenberg, Photo Researchers

Printed in the United States of America.
1 2 3 4 5 6 7 8 9 10 99 98 97 96 95
ISBN: 0-8359-4634-7
C44

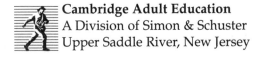 **Cambridge Adult Education**
A Division of Simon & Schuster
Upper Saddle River, New Jersey

Contents

Unit 3   Paragraphs   67

Unit
1

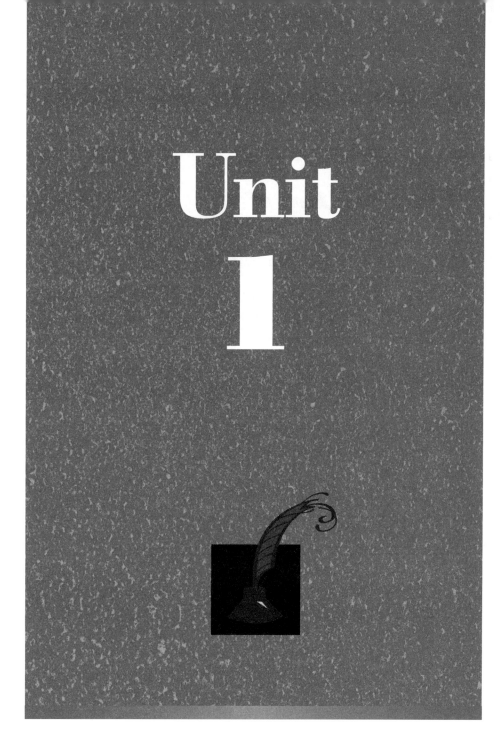

Words

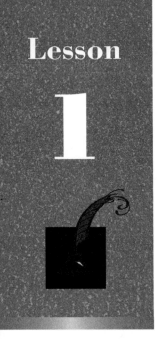

From Words to Sentences

What You Know   Have you ever listened to a message on an answering machine? Sometimes, the message comes through loud and clear: "This is Sonya. I am leaving my house now. Meet me downstairs in five minutes. We can walk to work together."

At other times, when the battery is dying, for example, the message is not so clear: "This is . . . I am . . . my house. . . . Meet me . . . in . . . minutes. We . . . together."

The second message doesn't make sense. The words are confusing. They don't express, or say, complete thoughts.

How It Works

You speak and write in order to get across your ideas. If what you say or write is confusing, people will not understand you. In order to get your ideas across, your words should express complete thoughts.

Here are three groups of words that do not give enough information to make sense.

left for class

Who left for class?

Willie wants

What does Willie *want*?

looking for a

Who is looking for *what*?

Can you add words to the examples to make them clear? Here are some ways you could do it:

Donna left for class.

Willie wants a new coat.

John is looking for a book.

Try It

The audience is enjoying what the speaker is saying. He is getting across his ideas.

One of the groups of words below expresses a complete thought. The other is confusing. Circle the group of words that makes sense.

took the books back to the library

Bob bought paint.

The second group of words makes sense. It tells who is doing something.

In the first group of words, you don't know *who* took the books back to the library. Add one or more words to make the first example less confusing.

_____ took the books back to the library.

You could write any person's name here. You could also write, "I took the books back to the library."

Here's another example. Circle the group of words that is confusing.

The tenant paid her rent.

The painter painting

The second group of words is confusing. You need a word that links *painter* to *painting*. Add one or more words to make the second example less confusing.

The painter *is* painting.

This is one way you can link *painter* to *painting*.

Practice

Add words to each group of words below so that they make sense.

1. _____ learned to drive.

2. Harry took _____.

3. _____ at the office.

4. Georgia arrived at the _____.

5. She will _____.

6. _____ works at his desk.

7. _____ after work.

8. The telephone _____.

9. _____ is fixing the _____.

10. _____ in the car.

Check your answers on page 113.

Follow-Up

Here is part of a telephone message. Many words are missing. Add words so that the message makes sense. If there are others doing this activity, compare your message with theirs. You may be surprised at how many different ways the message can be written.

This is Chris. I'll meet you at _____ o'clock in front of _____.

Be sure to _____.

Singular Nouns

What You Know Look around you. What do you
see? Most likely you are sitting on a <u>chair</u> as you read this <u>book</u>.
You may be next to a <u>friend</u>. Maybe a <u>teacher</u> is in the <u>room</u>.
Are you feeling <u>interest</u>? <u>Boredom</u>?

How It Works

Look carefully at the underlined words above:

chair	book	friend	teacher
boredom	room	interest	

Each word is a noun. A **noun** names a person, place, thing,
feeling, or idea. Here are some more examples of nouns:

Person: Quincy Jones, athlete, woman

Place: Atlantic Ocean, river, desert

Thing: desk, waterfall, Golden Gate Bridge

Feeling: pain, boredom, excitement

Idea: freedom, honesty, liberty

Nouns can be singular or plural. **Singular** means one thing
or idea. **Plural** means more than one. Here are more examples of
singular nouns:

The *carpenter* arrived at 9 AM.

A *hammer* is on the *bench*.

A *screwdriver* is on the *floor*.

You will learn more about plural nouns in Lesson 3.

Try It

Nouns can be found everywhere, even in the classroom. How many singular nouns can you find in this picture?

Circle the three *singular* nouns in this sentence:

Nate built the table and bookcase.

The three singular nouns in the sentence are *Nate*, *table*, and *bookcase*. Each names one person, place, or thing. Read these words out loud.

Now read the two sentences below. Can you find the seven singular nouns? Circle the *singular* nouns.

Hector ordered a stapler and a lamp.

A computer, a desk, and a chair are in the office.

The singular nouns are *Hector*, *stapler*, *lamp*, *computer*, *desk*, *chair*, and *office*. Read these words out loud.

Practice

Read the following sentences. Then circle the *singular* nouns.

1. Clyde works as a waiter in a restaurant.

2. George is the cook.

3. Before the restaurant opens, George often eats a hamburger.

4. Clyde has a steak and a baked potato.

5. One day, George made a special dessert.

6. Ethel and Julia tasted the pie.

7. Ms. Rodriguez ordered the dessert.

8. A smile was on her face.

9. Ms. Rodriguez asked to shake the hand of the cook.

10. The pie was the bestselling item on the menu.

Check your answers on page 113.

Follow-Up

Look around you. Make a list of all of the things that you see that are nouns. How many *singular* nouns can you find?

Plural Nouns

What You Know

Is there one window, or are there several <u>windows</u>, where you are now? Is there one chair, or are there many <u>chairs</u>? Maybe there is one desk, or maybe there are a few *desks*. Are you the only student? Maybe there are other <u>students</u> as well.

How It Works

All the underlined words above are examples of **plural nouns**. *Plural* means more than one. A *plural noun* names more than one person, place, thing, feeling, or idea. Here are more examples of plural nouns:

dogs	boxes	offices	bushes
students	pains	freedoms	

To make most nouns plural, add *s* or *es* to the end of the singular noun.

The *carpenter* arrived on time.

The *carpenter<u>s</u>* arrived on time.

The singular noun *carpenter* is made plural by adding *s*.

A *hammer* is on the *bench*.

Hammer<u>s</u> are on the *bench<u>es</u>*.

The singular word *hammer* is made plural by adding *s*. The singular word *bench* is made plural by adding *es*.

To make nouns plural that end in a consonant followed by *y*, change the *y* to *i* and add *es*:

Singular	Plural
fly	flies
strawberry	strawberries
city	cities

How many plural nouns can you find in this picture?

Nouns ending in a vowel followed by *y* can be made plural by leaving the *y* in and adding *s*.

Singular	**Plural**
monkey	monkeys
turkey	turkeys
boy	boys

Try It

Read this sentence. Circle the three plural nouns.

The students brought pens and pencils to the test.

The plural nouns are *students, pens,* and *pencils. Students* are more than one *person. Pens* and *pencils* are more than one *thing.*

Now read the sentence below. There are two plural nouns and one singular noun in it. Circle the plural nouns. Underline the singular noun.

There were 16 chairs and four tables in the room.

The plural nouns are *chairs* and *tables.* The singular noun is *room.*

Fill in the blank spaces with plural nouns.

In the forest, Amanda saw three _____ and many

_____ .

Amanda may have seen three *bears* or many *trees.* Whatever Amanda saw, they were *plural.* You know this because you see the words *three* and *many.*

9

Practice

Underline the *plural* nouns in each of the following sentences.

1. Jolene fixes cars.

2. She looks carefully at the engines.

3. Sometimes, the pistons need cleaning.

4. Often, the rings need to be changed.

5. The valves can be very dirty.

6. Jolene walks around the cars checking the tires.

7. The treads on some tires are worn.

8. Mufflers can cause problems.

9. The brakes sometimes need to be fixed or replaced.

10. Usually, the radios work quite well.

Check your answers on page 113.

Follow-Up

If there is a window in the room you are in, look outside. Give yourself about one minute to list as many things as you can see that are plural nouns.

Pronouns

What You Know   Read this sentence. Does it sound strange to you?

> As Jerry walked Jerry's dog, Jerry talked with Jerry's friend Eduardo.

The sentence probably sounds silly because the word *Jerry* is repeated so many times.

Here's the sentence again. Only this time, the word *Jerry* is replaced some of the time.

> As Jerry walked his dog, he talked with his friend Eduardo.

How It Works

The underlined words above are all examples of **pronouns**. A pronoun is a word that takes the place of a noun. Without pronouns, the same nouns would have to be used over and over. The result would be sentences that sound as strange as this one:

> When Don finished eating Don's lunch, Don put what was left of Don's lunch in Don's backpack.

When the sentence is rewritten using pronouns, it sounds much better:

> When Don finished eating *his* lunch, *he* put what was left of *it* in *his* backpack.

Here are more examples of pronouns:

She tossed the ball to *him*.

They watched *us* as *we* left.

I told *her* about *you*.

We gave *them* our address.

Ronnie is *their* brother.

11

All the people and things in this photograph can be named by nouns. They also can be named by pronouns. How many pronouns can you use to stand in for nouns?

Try It

Read the two sentences below. Underline the sentence that sounds better.

Haley bought Haley's friend some lunch.

Haley bought her friend some lunch.

The second sentence sounds better because the pronoun *her* is used to replace the noun *Haley's*.

Pete and Pat put on their rollerblades.

Pete and Pat put on Pete and Pat's rollerblades.

In this example, the first sentence sounds better because the pronoun *their* replaces the nouns *Pete's* and *Pat's*.

Victoria took her license out of her wallet.

Victoria took Victoria's license out of Victoria's wallet.

The first sentence sounds better because the pronoun *her* replaces the noun *Victoria's*.

Practice

Underline the pronouns in each of the following sentences.

1. Please send me a letter.

2. She is going to the beach this summer.

3. Did you receive their postcard?

4. That is his house.

5. Where is your brother?

6. They gave her a ride to the park.

7. Jeff tossed the ball to him.

8. Tanya left the keys for us.

9. Please meet our cousins from Florida.

10. The tree has lost its leaves.

Check your answers on page 114.

Follow-Up

A **proverb** is a saying that gives advice or states a truth. Many proverbs have pronouns in them. Here are three proverbs. Underline the pronouns. Then write what you think each proverb means.

A fool and his money are soon parted.

Three may keep a secret if two of them are dead.

When the well's dry, we know the worth of water.

Adjectives

What You Know   Think about one of your friends. Is she <u>tall</u> or <u>short</u>? Is he <u>messy</u> or <u>neat</u>? Is she <u>funny</u>, <u>kind</u>, <u>shy</u>, or <u>daring</u>? Is he <u>lazy</u>, <u>energetic</u>, <u>friendly</u>, <u>happy</u>, or <u>sad</u>? How many different words can you think of to describe your friend?

How It Works

All the underlined words above describe the noun *friend*. A word that describes a noun is called an **adjective**. Adjectives tell *what kind*, *how much* or *how many*, or *which one* or *which ones*.

> Justina is a *happy* camper. (*What kind* of camper?)
>
> We received *some* mail. (*How much* mail?)
>
> Frank has *two* jobs. (*How many* jobs?)
>
> Herman brought *these* packages. (*Which* packages?)

The adjectives used most often are called **articles**. They are *a*, *an*, and *the*.

> Can you find *a* map? (Use *a* when it comes before a word starting with a consonant.)
>
> Ralph will take *an* exam. (Use *an* when it comes before a word starting with a vowel.)
>
> Georgia is now *the* boss.

Here's an example of all three articles in one sentence.

> *An* orange, *a* pear, and some grapes are in *the* fruit bowl.

Some adjectives go in front of the nouns they describe.

> *Honest* Abe was well-known throughout the land.

Other adjectives are placed after the nouns they describe.

> Abe Lincoln was *honest*.

Look at Abe Lincoln in this picture. How many adjectives can you think of to describe him?

Try It

There is one adjective in each sentence below (*not* including articles). Circle the adjective in each sentence.

Abraham Lincoln wore a tall hat.

He had a long beard.

He was a thin man.

The adjective in the first sentence is *tall*. It describes the word *hat*. The adjective in the second sentence is *long*. It describes the word *beard*. The adjective in the third sentence is *thin*. It describes the word *man*.

There are five adjectives in the sentences below (*not* including articles). Can you find them?

Abraham Lincoln was the sixteenth president.

He was known as honest Abe.

Lincoln was a good husband, a caring father, and a great president.

The five adjectives are *sixteenth, honest, good, caring,* and *great*. Read the sentences out loud.

Practice

Read the following sentences. Then circle all the adjectives—including articles. The number in parentheses following each sentence tells you how many adjectives are in that sentence.

1. Tanya and Paul have saved some money. (1)

2. They will buy a new house. (2)

3. The brick house is on a dirt road. (4)

4. It was built three months ago. (1)

5. The house has three bedrooms and two bathrooms. (3)

6. It also has a beautiful porch and a large den. (4)

7. The yard is big. (2)

8. Tanya has chosen green carpet for the large bedroom and a yellow rug for the small bedroom. (7)

9. Paul picked out a brown sofa and a black chair. (4)

10. Tanya and Paul will move in early September. (1)

Check your answers on page 114.

Follow-Up

How many different adjectives can you think of to describe the room you are in now? Give yourself one minute to come up with as many adjectives as you can. If other people are doing this activity, compare your adjectives with theirs.

Verbs

What You Know   Do you know how to make scrambled eggs? Can you explain how to do it to a friend who doesn't know how to cook? You probably can. Suppose that you had to explain it using only nouns and adjectives? Could you do it then? You would end up with a bunch of unconnected words —two eggs, frying pan, butter, stove, bowl, salt, pepper, a little milk, fork, and so on. What's missing here is the action.

How It Works

Look at these sentences.

<u>Take</u> two eggs and <u>break</u> them into a bowl.

<u>Add</u> a little milk, salt, and pepper.

<u>Mix</u> the eggs.

<u>Put</u> a frying pan on the stove.

<u>Melt</u> some butter in the pan.

<u>Pour</u> the eggs into the pan.

<u>Stir</u> the eggs with a fork as they <u>cook</u>.

All the underlined words have one thing in common. They all show action. Words that show action are called **verbs**.

You may have chosen other verbs to explain how to make scrambled eggs. Here is the sentence *Mix the eggs* with a different verb choice.

Beat the eggs.

Now look at the sentence *Melt some butter in the pan*. Think of another verb to use instead of *melt*. Write it on the blank below.

_____ some butter in the pan.

You could have said *heat* the butter or *cook* the butter. Both these words show action.

Try It

Circle the word in this sentence that shows action.

The player jogs onto the court.

The word that shows action is *jogs*. It tells how the player moves.
There are two action words in this sentence. Circle them.

The crowd waves and cheers.

The two verbs are *waves* and *cheers*. Each shows an action.
Now here's a sentence with three verbs. Circle them.

The player runs, shoots, and scores.

The verbs are *runs, shoots,* and *scores*. These words show action.

Look at the action in this picture. How many verbs can you think of to express the action that is taking place?

UNIT 1   Words

Practice

Circle the verb in each sentence.

1. The referee threw the ball into the air.

2. Two players jumped high.

3. Michael bounced the ball to a teammate.

4. Patrick dribbled the ball down the court.

5. He moved quickly.

6. He passed the ball to another player.

7. John caught the ball.

8. He raced to the basket.

9. He leaped into the air.

10. John slammed the ball into the basket.

Check your answers on page 114.

Follow-Up

Announcers of sporting events know many different words to describe the action that is taking place. For example, a person announcing a baseball game might say that a player *ran* or *raced* to first base.

Imagine that you are the announcer at a sporting event. It could be a hockey game, a baseball game, a soccer game, a tennis match, or any other sporting event. Think of at least three different verbs to describe one action that takes place during the game.

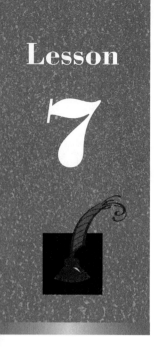

Adverbs

What You Know
Imagine that you are a reporter at a fire. You might write these sentences about the event.

The fire raced <u>quickly</u> through the house.

The firefighters fought <u>bravely</u>.

They <u>carefully</u> entered the burning building.

One firefighter <u>slowly</u> helped a person down the ladder.

How It Works
Each underlined word above describes a verb in the sentence. Words that describe verbs are called **adverbs**. Adverbs often answer the questions *how often*? *how*? *where*? and *when*?

The lunch whistle blows *daily* at noon. (The word *daily* tells how often the whistle blows.)

The workers eat *quickly* in the lunchroom. (The word *quickly* tells how the workers eat.)

They eat *there* every day. (The word *there* tells where they eat.)

Then they go back to work. (The word *then* tells when they go back to work.)

Adverbs can come after the verbs they describe.

The whistle blows *loudly* at the factory. (The word *loudly* is an adverb that describes how the whistle *blows*.)

Adverbs can come before the verbs they describe.

People *usually* hear it all over town. (The word *usually* is an adverb that describes the verb *hear*.)

Did you notice that many adverbs end in *ly*? Most words that end in *ly* are adverbs.

Imagine what you would do if you were in a forest. What animals might you see? What might they be doing? Use verbs to describe their actions. Use adverbs to describe the verbs.

Try It

Circle the adverb in this sentence:

> The bird sang loudly in the tree. (The word *loudly* is the adverb. It describes the verb *sang*. It tells *how* the bird sang.)

There are two adverbs in the sentence below. Can you find them? Circle them.

> Susie turned slowly and quietly in the woods. (The two adverbs are *slowly* and *quietly*. They both describe the verb *turned*. They tell *how* Susie turned.)

Can you think of one different adverb to replace the two adverbs in the sentence above? Write the whole sentence with the new adverbs on the line below.

_____

_____

Practice

Read the following sentences. There is one adverb in each sentence. Circle each adverb.

1. Connie types quickly.

2. She types accurately.

3. She does her work carefully.

4. Connie slowly reads a report about car safety.

5. She agrees totally with everything it says.

6. Some people drive fast.

7. They drive carelessly.

8. They may drive recklessly.

9. Connie drove home slowly.

10. She arrived safely.

Check your answers on page 114.

Follow-Up

Think of your favorite singer. Make a list of words to describe how this singer sings.

More Adverbs

What You Know   You've just been to the best
movie you have ever seen. You want to tell your family about it.
Words like good or great just don't seem enough. You might say,
"It was very good. It was really great!" You use extra words to
help you explain your thoughts.

How It Works

In the last lesson, you learned that adverbs describe verbs. In
this lesson, you will learn how adverbs can describe adjectives
or other adverbs.

> The office manager needs workers who can work *very* quickly.
> (The word *quickly* is an adverb that describes how the
> work is done. The word *very* is an adverb that describes
> *quickly*. It explains *how* quickly the workers work.)

Now read this sentence.

> The manager interviewed a *fairly* smart worker. (The word
> *smart* is an adjective. It describes the worker. The word
> *fairly* describes *smart*. It tells you that the worker wasn't
> really smart or too smart. The worker was "medium
> smart." It helps make the meaning of *smart* clearer.)

The manager interviews someone who wants a job.

23

Try It

There is one adverb in the sentence below. Circle it.

Vinnie bought a very powerful car. (The adverb is *very*. It gives more information about the adjective *powerful*. It tells *how* powerful the car is.)

There are two adverbs in the sentence below. Circle them both.

The car drives quite smoothly. (The two adverbs are *quite* and *smoothly*. The word *quite* gives information about the adverb *smoothly*. It tells *how* smoothly the car drives.)

Practice

Circle the adverb or adverbs in each sentence.

1. Vinnie's car is too expensive for me.

2. However, the car is quite comfortable.

3. The engine is really powerful.

4. The radio is truly great.

5. The sound is very clear.

6. The color is pretty loud.

7. It is unusually bright.

8. Vinnie drives rather quickly.

9. He is an extremely safe driver.

10. The car must last a very long time.

Check your answers on page 114.

Follow-Up

Think about how you dance. Use the words *very* and *fairly* to describe your dancing.

The Present Tense

What You Know Imagine that you are in a classroom with several other students. What do they usually do? Here are some possibilities:

Stephen <u>walks</u> in the door.

He <u>sits</u> down in a chair in the front row.

Rita <u>says</u> hello.

They <u>smile</u> at each other.

How It Works

Each underlined verb above shows action that happens all the time, or on a regular basis. These verbs are said to be in the **present tense**. The word *tense* means *time*.

Verbs in the present tense may also show action that happens today. For example:

Elise *arrives* at the office on time.

Someone *hands* her several sheets of paper.

She *fills* out the forms.

She *writes* carefully.

Elise *waits* to be called for her interview.

Read these two sentences. The underlined words are both in the present tense. Can you tell which shows the present and which shows something that happens all the time?

Elise <u>stands</u> when she hears someone call her name.

Elise <u>feels</u> nervous at job interviews.

The first sentence shows something that is happening in the present: *Elise stands*. The second sentence shows something that happens all the time at job interviews: *Elise feels nervous*.

Describe what is taking place in the photograph by using verbs in the present tense.

Try It

Each sentence below has one verb that is in the present tense. Circle each of these.

> The judge enters the courtroom.
>
> Everyone stands.
>
> The judge takes his seat.
>
> Then everyone else sits, too.
>
> The trial begins.

The verbs are *enters, stands, takes, sits,* and *begins.* They all show action that is taking place in the present.

Can you think of a verb in the present tense for the sentence below? Write it in the answer blank.

> The lawyer _____ in a clear voice.

One possible answer is *speaks.* Another is *talks.* Did you think of a different verb?

Practice

Find the present tense verb in each sentence. Write the verb on the answer blank at the end of each sentence.

1. The trial begins at 9 A.M. _____

2. The jury walks into the courtroom. _____

3. Some people whisper. _____

4. A photographer takes some pictures. _____

5. A lawyer walks up to the judge. _____

6. She speaks softly. _____

7. The judge listens. _____

8. No one in the courtroom moves. _____

9. The lawyer returns to her seat. _____

10. The judge sends everyone home for the day. _____

Check your answers on page 114.

Follow-Up

Have you ever heard the expression, "I wish I were a fly on the wall"? It means that you wish you could be in a room but not be seen by anyone. That way, you could see and hear what is taking place without anyone knowing.

Imagine that you are a fly on the wall now in a kitchen where a water pipe has just broken. You watch as each event takes place. Write five sentences describing what happens as it is happening. Use one present tense verb in each sentence. Here are some possible examples:

Water *squirts* everywhere. The walls and ceiling *get* wet. The water *lands* on top of the stove.

The Present Continuous Tense

What You Know

Right now, this minute, you are reading this book. What else are you doing right now? You are breathing. You are sitting. You are thinking. When something is happening right now, you use a verb tense that shows "right now."

How It Works

Some verbs tell of actions that take place right now. These verbs are in the **present continuous tense**.

The present continuous tense is made up of two verbs. The first one is the present tense of *to be*. Here are the different ways to say *to be* in the present tense:

I *am*	we *are*
you *are* (one person)	you *are* (more than one person)
he, she, or it *is*	they *are*
singular noun *is*	plural nouns *are*

The second verb that makes up the present continuous tense is the one that explains the action. Take this word and add *ing*, for example, read*ing*, see*ing*, go*ing*, and think*ing*.

Sometimes, when *ing* is added, the spelling of the word changes a bit. Here are some examples:

have + ing = having	change + ing = changing
serve + ing = serving	run + ing = running

Now put the two verbs together.

The waiter *is serving* the coffee.

The action is in the present and is still happening. The words *is* (present tense of *to be*) and *serving* (serve + ing) make up the present continuous tense.

Try It

Look at the children in the picture. Describe what they are doing by using verbs in the present continuous tense.

Read this sentence. Circle the verbs in the present continuous tense.

Bonnie is taking her children to the park.

The present continuous tense in this sentence is *is taking*. It is the present tense of *to be* and *take + ing*. It shows that the action is happening right now.

Circle the present continuous tense in this example:

The children are playing on the swings. (The present continuous tense is *are playing*. It shows action that is happening in the present.)

The following sentence shows the present tense. Change the present tense to the present continuous tense. Write your answer on the answer blank.

Bonnie sits on a bench. _____

The correct answer is *is sitting. Is sitting* puts *is* (the present tense of to be) together with *sit + ing*. It shows action that is happening now.

Try this again. Change the present tense to the present continuous.

She watches the children. _____

The correct answer is *is watching*. The action is happening now.

Practice 1

Read the following sentences. Then circle the verbs in the present continuous tense.

1. Several people are applying for the job.

2. They are filling out forms now.

3. They are hoping to become store managers.

4. The present manager is leaving to open a store in Ohio.

5. The clothing store is looking for bright, young people.

Practice 2

The verbs in the following sentences are in the present tense. Change them to the present continuous tense. Write your answers on the answer blanks.

1. All the applicants look for work. _____

2. Several work at other jobs. _____

3. One person asks to borrow a pen. _____

4. Another person thinks about his family. _____

5. Everyone waits nervously for an interview. _____

Check your answers on page 115.

Follow-Up

Write five sentences telling of things that are happening right now. Circle the verbs in the present continuous tense. You could have a sentence like this:

I *am watching* Victor write his sentences.

The Past Tense

What You Know   Have you ever had a baby-sitting job? If so, you probably <u>played</u> several games with the child. Maybe you <u>listened</u> to some music. If you were lucky, you <u>watched</u> the child sleep soundly. At the end of the evening, you probably <u>received</u> some money.

How It Works

All the underlined verbs above tell of actions that took place in the past. The actions are no longer happening. They are over. These are verbs in the **past tense**. Here are some more examples of verbs that show action that took place in the past.

> Henry <u>worked</u> late last night.

> He <u>fixed</u> a stereo.

> His partner <u>checked</u> the cash register.

Each underlined word tells of an action that took place in the past. These words are all in the past tense.

Many past tense verbs are formed by adding *d* or *ed* to the present tense verb.

Present Tense	Past Tense
laugh	laughed
shave	shaved
invite	invited

To form the past tense of verbs that end in *y*, change the *y* to *i* and add *ed*.

Present Tense	Past Tense
cry	cried
try	tried

Try It

Suppose this storm took place yesterday. You would have to use verbs in the past tense to describe what happened.

Only one of these sentences has a past tense verb in it. Circle the past tense verb.

> Lightning is flashing in the sky.

> Lightning flashed in the sky.

The second sentence has the past tense verb *flashed* in it. The first sentence has a verb in the present continuous tense. The verb *is flashing* is in the present continuous tense.
Can you find the sentence with a past tense verb in it? Circle the one you think it is.

> The sky is darkening to black.

> The sky darkened to black.

The second sentence has a past tense verb in it. The past tense verb is *darkened*.

Practice

In each sentence below, the verb is missing. Choose the past tense verb from the choices given in parentheses. Write the verb in the answer blank.

1. Last year, Jean and I _____ to New York City. (traveled, are traveling)

2. We _____ the Empire State Building, the Statue of Liberty, and the World Trade Center. (visit, visited)

3. I _____ in many different stores. (shopped, will shop)

4. We _____ the city in a bus. (tour, toured)

5. Jean _____ down many streets in Greenwich Village. (will walk, walked)

6. He especially _____ visiting Rockefeller Center. (liked, likes)

7. We _____ lots of different kinds of food. (are tasting, tasted)

8. I _____ our visit to Lincoln Center. (enjoys, enjoyed)

9. We _____ while a movie was being filmed in the street. (watched, watching)

10. Jean _____ the South Street Seaport. (admired, admiring)

Check your answers on page 115.

Follow-Up

Here are six verbs in the past tense: looked, waited, hoped, prayed, cheered, raced. Write a paragraph about an event that made you afraid. Use at least four of the past tense verbs from the list and underline them.

The Future Tense

What You Know   Some people like to make plans. They use sentences like these:

In five years, I will work as a teacher.

I will teach third graders.

My family will live in a bigger apartment.

I will earn a lot of money.

Can you think of something you would like to be doing in five years? Write this in the answer blank.

I will _____.

How It Works

The underlined words above show actions that will take place in the future. Together, the two words underlined form the **future tense**.

To form the future tense, use the word *will* before the verb. Here are some examples:

I *will read* to the students.

They *will listen* carefully.

Everyone *will learn* how to add, subtract, multiply, and divide.

The children *will enjoy* my class.

All the verbs talk about things that haven't happened yet. They talk about the future.

Try It

Ben Franklin was, among other things, a famous inventor.

Read the five sentences below about Ben Franklin. Circle the one sentence that has a future tense verb.

Ben Franklin wanted to be a sailor.

Instead, he learned the printing trade.

He invented many things, such as the Franklin stove.

He helped write the Declaration of Independence.

He will stay alive forever with his picture on the $100 bill.

Only the last sentence has a future tense verb. It is *will stay*. The other sentences are written in the past tense.

Read these sentences about one of Ben's inventions. One of the sentences is in the future tense. Circle the right one.

Ben discovered that he needed reading glasses.

He invented bifocals.

Bifocals are divided into two parts.

The top part is for reading, and the bottom part is for seeing things far away.

People will think of Ben whenever they put on their glasses.

The last sentence is in the future tense. The verb *will think* is a future tense verb.

Practice

Circle the future tense verbs in the sentences below.

1. Next week, we will visit Washington, D.C.

2. First, we will tour the White House.

3. Then, we will walk to the Lincoln Memorial.

4. My sister will photograph the statue of Lincoln.

5. Next, we will see the Washington Monument.

6. My sister, my brother, and I will read the names on the Vietnam Memorial.

7. My brother will buy several souvenirs.

8. I will ride past the Capitol building.

9. We will drive around the city at night.

10. The lights will shine on all the monuments.

Check your answers on page 115.

Follow-Up

Plan a trip. Imagine that you can go anywhere in the world. Where will you go? What will you see? Write at least five sentences using verbs in the future tense to describe things you will do.

Unit
2

Sentences

What Is a Sentence?

What You Know   We've all heard people talk on the phone. We only hear half of the conversation. It might sound like this:

> Yes . . . Sure . . . Okay . . . No, what about 7:30? Fine . . . See you then. Bye.

When we talk to someone, it's fine to answer in one or two words. Even over the phone, you are both "there" to speak, listen, ask questions, make things clearer, and do all the other things we do when we have a conversation.

Writing is different. It's a one-way conversation. No one else is there to ask questions, make a statement, or tell you that what you are saying is clear. For this reason, what you write must be easy to understand, clear, and complete.

When you write, words are your tools. You wouldn't use a hammer to tighten a bolt. In the same way, you shouldn't use a noun when you should use a verb. It wouldn't get the job done. Your "job" in writing is to get your thoughts, ideas, and information across to the people who read what you write. When you put the right words together, you form sentences.

How It Works

Sentences are groups of words that tell complete thoughts. Here are three sample sentences:

1. The exam begins at 9 A.M. tomorrow.

2. You must arrive on time.

3. A teacher will tell you which room to go to.

Notice that each sentence begins with a *capital letter*: The, You, and A. Each sentence ends with a *period* (.). The capital letter tells you where the sentence begins. The period tells you where the sentence ends.

Look at what is happening in the picture. Use complete sentences to describe what you see.

Try It

Read the two groups of words below about life in North America in the 1700s and 1800s. Only one group is a sentence. Circle the right one.

Abraham Lincoln was President during the Civil War.

George Washington the first President.

The first group of words is a sentence. It begins with a capital letter. It ends with a period. It expresses a complete thought. The other group of words does not express a complete thought.

In the second group of words, you wonder about the relationship between George Washington and the first President. Here are the words so that they make a sentence:

George Washington was the first president.

Circle the group of words below that is a sentence.

People traveled to America to seek freedom.

wanted adventure

The first group of words is a sentence. It begins with a capital letter and ends with a period. The most important thing is that it expresses a complete thought.

Practice

Some of the groups of words below express complete thoughts.
Others do not. If a group expresses a complete thought, rewrite
it on the blank line. Make sure it begins with a capital letter and
ends with a period. If the group of words does not express a
complete thought, add words of your own to make it a sentence.
Then write your sentence on the answer blank.

1. my friend Willie is a bus driver _____

_____

2. he goes to work at 7 A.M. every weekday _____

_____

3. on weekends _____

_____

4. he driving an old bus _____

_____

5. he has never had an accident _____

_____

6. Willie always tries hard to _____

_____

7. he was voted the most helpful bus driver _____

_____

8. he the award on the dashboard _____

_____

Check your answers on page 115.

Follow-Up

Some song titles are complete sentences. For example, "Someday We'll Be
Together." Think of five song titles that are complete sentences. Write them
on a sheet of paper.

What Sentences Can Do

What You Know   In the morning, most homes are busy places. People are rushing to go to school and work. Someone may be preparing breakfast. Everyone seems to have something to say:

MANUEL: I would like a strong cup of coffee.
GRACE: Where's the milk?
MARIA: Come to the table right now.
MARIO: I don't want pancakes!

Notice how each person expresses his or her ideas in a different way. Hector tells what he wants. Grace asks a question. Maria gives a command. Mario shows strong feelings.

How It Works

Sentences can do different things to help you get your ideas across. All the thoughts about breakfast above are expressed in a different kind of sentence. There are four kinds:

1. Some sentences make a statement. These sentences then end with a *period* (.).

I would like some tea.   Ramon is still sleeping.

2. Some sentences ask a question. They end with a *question mark* (?).

Where's the milk?   Have you seen Matty?

3. Some sentences make a request or give a command. They usually end with a period. Sometimes they end with an *exclamation point* (!). These sentences are said to "you." The *you* is never stated. They often begin with a verb.

Come to the table right now!   Please move over.

4. Some sentences show strong feeling. They end with an *exclamation point*.

I don't like pancakes!   This is awful!

Try It

Each sentence below is an example of one of the four kinds of sentences. Write S next to the sentence that makes a statement. Write Q next the one that asks a question. Write C next to the sentence that gives a command. Write F next to the one that shows strong feelings.

Tito moved into a new apartment.

Do you know where it is?

He's the luckiest person in the world!

Drive us there now.

Which sentence makes a statement? (The first sentence does: *Tito moved into a new apartment.* It makes a statement and ends with a period.)

Which sentence asks a question? (The second sentence does: *Do you know where it is?* It asks a question. It ends with a question mark.)

Which sentence makes a request or gives a command? (The last sentence does: *Drive us there now.* It gives a command. It ends with a period.)

Which sentence shows strong feeling? (The third sentence does: *He's the luckiest person in the world!* It shows strong feeling. It ends with an exclamation point.)

Write four sentences about things that are taking place in this picture. Write one of each different kind of sentence—make a statement, ask a question, make a request or give a command, and show strong feeling.

Practice

There is no end mark in any of the groups of words below. Add the correct end mark. Then write what kind of sentence each is: makes a statement, asks a question, makes a request or gives a command, or shows strong feeling.

1. My apartment is not in good condition _____

2. Have you seen the walls _____

3. Come and take a look _____

4. This is terrible _____

5. I've called the landlord three times _____

6. He is always too busy to answer the phone _____

7. Everything is leaking _____

8. I can't stand it another minute _____

9. Do you think I can sue him _____

10. Please help me right away _____

Check your answers on page 116.

Follow-Up

Find the title of a book. It can be any book at all. Add or change some words in the title to form four different kinds of sentences, a sentence that makes a statement, asks a question, makes a request or gives a command, or shows strong feeling. Here's an example:

Book title: *The Color Purple*
Statement: I like the color purple.
Question: Do you like the color purple?
Command: Give me the purple-colored marker.
Strong feeling: I can't stand the color purple!

Subjects

What You Know

Can you think of a movie you have seen that doesn't have a star in it? The star usually plays the leading role. This is the person the movie is all about. In a way, subjects play the leading role in sentences. They are what the sentence is all about.

How It Works

Every sentence needs a **subject**. A **subject** tells the person, place, or thing about which something is said. The subject tells *who* or *what* the sentence is about. A group of words without a subject cannot be a sentence. This is because, without a subject, the sentence cannot express a complete thought.

Look at these song titles:

"Back in My Arms Again"
"Leaving Las Vegas"
"Stuck On You"

None of these titles expresses a complete thought. None is a sentence. None has a subject. Here's the first song title with a subject added: *Nick is back in my arms again.* Can you make a complete thought out of the other two titles?

To find the subject of a sentence, ask yourself: *who* or *what* is the sentence about? *Who* or *what* is doing something or is something happening to? Here are two examples:

Wanda pays the bills.   The bills just keep coming.

In both sentences you can ask: What is this sentence about? In the first sentence, you ask: *Who* is doing something? *Wanda* is. She is paying the bills. *Wanda* is the subject of the sentence.

In the second sentence, you ask: *What* just keeps coming? The *bills*, of course, is the subject.

Did you notice that the subject of both sentences is a noun? You learned about nouns in Lessons 2 and 3. The subject of almost all sentences is a noun or a pronoun. You learned about pronouns in Lesson 4. Now you can see why nouns and pronouns are so important.

Does this look like a video store in your neighborhood? Write two sentences about what you see in the picture. Each sentence should have a different subject.

Try It

Read these sentences. Circle the subject of each one.

Sharon works in a video store.

People rent videos all day and all night.

Videos have to be returned within two days.

The first sentence is about *Sharon*. She is the subject. *Who* is working in a video store? *Sharon* is working in a video store.

The second sentence is about *people* who rent videos. *Who* rents videos? *People* rent videos.

The third sentence is about *videos*. *Videos* are what have to be returned. They are the subject of the sentence.

Here are two more sentences about the video store. Circle the subject in each one.

The store stays open until midnight on Saturday.

The manager works hard.

To find the subject of the first sentence, ask yourself *who* or *what* is the sentence about. It is about the *store*. *The store* stays open until midnight.

To find the subject of the second sentence, ask yourself again *who* or *what* is the sentence about? The subject of the second sentence is *the manager*. *Who* works hard? *The manager* works hard.

Practice 1

Circle the subject of each sentence.

1. Ida exercises every day.
2. Her muscles have grown.
3. Paul goes to a gym.
4. Swimming is his favorite sport.
5. Henry lifts weights.
6. Maria likes to jog.
7. Jogging gives her energy.
8. I enjoy volley ball.
9. Serving is my favorite part.
10. Exercising is fun.

Practice 2

Add a subject to each group of words below to form a sentence. Write your subject on the answer blank.

1. _____ is my favorite month.

2. _____ barks at fire trucks.

3. _____ will baby-sit for my daughter tonight.

4. _____ sings better than anyone else.

5. _____ studies with Vanessa.

Check your answers on page 116.

Follow-Up

Think of the names of five of your friends. Use each of their names as the subject in a sentence that tells something that person likes to do. For example:

Andrea plays the drums in a band.

Subjects and Verbs

What You Know   In the movie discussed in Lesson 15, we said the star had the leading role. However, even a star can't stand to have nothing to do. Every movie needs action. Something has to happen.

How It Works

Does the word *action* remind you of something you learned earlier in this book? In Lesson 6 you learned that *verbs* show action. In sentences, verbs tell what the subject is, does, is doing, did, or will do. Verbs may also tell what is done to the subject. Every sentence must have a subject and a verb.

In Lesson 13 you learned that a sentence is a group of words that expresses a complete thought. We can now add to that: *A sentence is a group of words that contains a subject and a verb and expresses a complete thought.* For example:

Sammi is driving.   Marlene runs.

Hakeem played.   They will speak.

Each of these groups has a subject and a verb and expresses a complete thought. Therefore, each is a sentence. Just a few words can be a sentence, just so long as the thought is complete.

Try It

Read the pairs of subjects and verbs below. Underline the pair that is a sentence (a complete thought).

1. Aleesha is crying.   **2.** Rain filled.

Pair 1 is the sentence. It expresses a complete thought. Even though pair 2 has a subject and verb, the thought is incomplete. You don't know what the rain filled. Pair 2 is not a sentence.

3. He bought.   **4.** They arrived.

Pair 4 is a sentence. It expresses a complete thought. Pair 3 does not. You don't know what he bought.

Practice

Read the pairs of subjects and verbs below. Underline the pairs that are sentences. Circle the ones that are not.

1. They are walking.

2. Nina dropped.

3. I like.

4. The suit looked.

5. Al sneezed.

6. Marva will work.

7. Luis sounds.

8. We are taking.

9. The cat wants.

10. The dog is sleeping.

Check your answers on page 116.

Follow-Up

Using only subjects and verbs, write three sentences about yourself. Each sentence should begin with the word *I*, which will be the subject of each sentence.

Thought Completers

What You Know   Imagine that you and your boyfriend or girlfriend are walking in the park. The night is cool. There is a full moon. You are having a wonderful time. Your friend takes your hand and looks into your eyes. This is what you hear:

> I love . . . .

Oh no! You missed the last word. Who or what does your friend love? These thoughts go through your mind:

> I love *you.*

> I love *your sweater.*

> I love *your eyes.*

> I love *Aunt Betty.*

> I love *a full moon.*

Which one did your friend say? What was missing? There was no word or words to complete the thought begun by your friend.

How It Works

You learned in Lesson 16 that a subject and verb do not always express a complete thought. For example:

> I love

> Henry bought

> They live

> Maurice likes

> He needs

These subjects and verbs leave you with questions. *Who* do I love? *What* did Henry buy? *Where* do they live? *What* does Maurice like? *What* does he need?

To make each of these subjects and verbs into a sentence, words are needed to complete the thought. A **thought completer** is a word or group of words that completes the thought begun by the subject and verb. Here are some examples:

I love <u>you</u>.

Henry bought <u>a new car</u>.

They live <u>near the lake</u>.

Maurice likes <u>swimming</u>.

He needs <u>to work</u>.

All the underlined words complete the thoughts begun by the subject and verb. They turn each group of words into a sentence.

Now look at these subjects and verbs.

| Sara feels | We were |
| The car looks | I am |

The verbs *feels*, *were*, *looks*, and *am* don't really show action. They say something about the subject and express what is or seems to be. They also link the subject to a thought completer. For example:

| Sara *feels* sick. | We *were* late. |
| The car *looks* clean. | I *am* happy to meet you. |

This is where cars are made. Look at the picture carefully. Write two sentences with nouns, verbs, and thought completers that tell about what you see in the picture.

Try It

Underline the thought completer in each sentence below.

Marge threw the ball to Ida.

Ida caught it.

The dog is black.

Bob went to the beach.

In the first sentence, the thought completer is *the ball to Ida*. In the second, the thought completer is *it*. In the third, the thought completer is *black*. In the last sentence, it is *to the beach*.

Practice

Underline the thought completer in each sentence.

1. Lila visited her relatives.
2. They live in Maine.
3. She traveled by bus.
4. The trip took 18 hours.
5. Lila loves to ride on buses.
6. She read an entire book.
7. She looked at the sights.
8. She closed her eyes to rest.
9. She ate a snack of crackers.
10. Lila enjoyed the trip.

Check your answers on page 117.

Follow-Up

Here are the titles of plays. Can you use them as the thought completers or as part of the thought completers in sentences of your own? *Ghosts, Our Town, The Seagull.*

Here's an example using the title of the play *Romeo and Juliet* as part of a thought completer:

I dropped off Romeo and Juliet at the movies.

Subject–Verb Agreement

What You Know Imagine reading this sentence in an ad from your local supermarket:

The peach are only three for $1

The person who wrote the ad made a mistake. Can you find it?

How It Works

In Lesson 2 you learned about singular nouns. You learned about plural nouns in Lesson 3. Pronouns also can be singular and plural.

Singular	Plural
I	we
you (one person)	you (more than one person)
he, she, it	they

Nouns and pronouns are the subjects of sentences. A verb that goes with a subject must be singular if the subject is singular. If a subject is plural, the verb must be plural. When this happens, the **subject and verb agree**.

Most of the time, it is easy to make a subject and verb agree because verbs don't change. Usually, verbs are the same whether they are singular or plural.

When do verbs change? Verbs change only in the present tense and only when the subject is *he, she, it,* or a *singular noun.* Then you add *s* or *es* to make the verb singular. (This is the opposite of the situation with nouns. To make a noun plural, you add an *s*.)

Let's take a look. The following examples show the verb *to like* in the present tense:

I like	we like
you like	you like
he, she, or it likes	they like
Mary likes	the cows like

He, *she*, *it*, and the singular noun *Mary* have the singular form of the verb *to like*, which is *likes*.

Here are some examples of different subjects and verbs. Remember: The *singular* form of a verb ends in *s*. The plural of each verb does not.

Singular	Plural
The girl plays.	The girls play.
She dances.	They dance.
The apple falls.	The apples fall.
The ball rolls.	The balls roll.

In some sentences, two or more nouns or pronouns can be the subject of the same verb. When this happens, the subjects are joined by *and* and are plural. These plural subjects require a plural verb. Here are some examples:

Jeremy and Jonah sing in a choir. (*Jeremy and Jonah* are the subjects of the plural verb *sing*.)

Tatiana and Troy dance. (*Tatiana and Troy* are the subjects of the plural verb *dance*.)

Look carefully at this picture. Here are subjects for two sentences about the picture. Complete the sentences by adding verbs and thought completers. Make sure the subject and the verb agree. The factory _____. The workers _____.

Try It

Each of the following sentences has a mistake in agreement between subject and verb. Circle the mistake in each one.

The moviegoers likes the movie.

In this sentence, the subject, *moviegoers*, is plural. The verb, *likes*, is singular. The sentence can be rewritten correctly this way:

The *moviegoers like* the movie.

My friend and I laughs during the funny parts.

In this sentence, there are two subjects: *my friend* and *I*. Plural subjects require a plural verb. The verb, *laughs*, is singular. The sentence can be rewritten correctly this way:

My friend and I laugh during the funny parts.

My friend enjoy every minute of it.

In this sentence, the subject is singular and the verb is plural. The sentence can be rewritten correctly this way:

My friend enjoys every minute of it.

Do you usually agree with your friends about the movies that you see together?

Practice

Some of the subjects and verbs below agree. Others do not. Write *correct* on the answer blank after the subjects and verbs that agree. If the subjects and verbs do not agree, write the correct verb on the answer blank.

1. Uri want a new TV. _____

2. Daisy likes to travel. _____

3. The students and teachers reads out loud. _____

4. The plumber fix the sink. _____

5. Beatrice call her mother every week. _____

6. The singers and actors hope for success. _____

7. The cats leap onto the sofa. _____

8. A swimmer dive in to the pool. _____

9. Her shoes squeak. _____

10. Radios and stereos plays too loud. _____

Check your answers on page 117.

Follow-Up

Write five sentences about how you feel about school. Circle all the subjects. Underline all the verbs. Make sure that all the subjects and verbs agree.

Choosing the Right Pronoun

What You Know Suppose you want to tell someone about yourself and your sister. Which statements might you make?

Me love to play soccer.   She plays goalie.

I love to play soccer.   Her plays goalie.

We practice Tuesday and Thursday evenings.

Us practice Tuesday and Thursday evenings.

Probably, you would choose these sentences:

I love to play soccer.   *She* plays goalie.

We practice Tuesday and Thursday evenings.

The other sentences might get across the ideas you want, but they don't follow the rules of written grammar.

How It Works

In Lesson 18, you learned the singular and plural forms of pronouns.

Singular	Plural
I	we
you	you
he, she, it	they

When you use a pronoun as a subject, you must *always* choose one of these pronouns. For example, you and one other person are going shopping. Fill in the correct pronoun:

_____ are going shopping.

The answer is *we*.

Pronouns also can be used as thought completers. If you use a pronoun as a thought completer, you must choose one of these pronouns:

Singular	Plural
me	us
you	you
him, her, it	them

Now let's look at all the pronouns to see how both kinds of pronouns work.

Subject Pronouns	Thought Completer Pronouns
I see Mike.	Mike sees *me*.
You see Mike.	Mike sees *you*.
He sees Mike.	Mike sees *him*.
She sees Mike.	Mike sees *her*.
It sees Mike.	Mike sees *it*.
We see Mike.	Mike sees *us*.
You (one person) see Mike.	Mike sees *you* (more than one person).
They see Mike.	Mike sees them.

Notice that *you* is the same whether it is singular or plural, and whether it is a subject or a thought completer. *It* is also the same as a subject and as a thought completer.

We make careful choices when we buy·clothes. We want the right thing to wear at the right time. For example, we wouldn't wear shorts and sneakers to church. We have to make careful choices with pronouns too. We have to use the right one at the right time.

Try It

Underline the correct subject pronoun in the sentences below.

She plays well.   Her plays well.

Them might win.   They might win.

Us are the winners.   We are the winners.

The correct subject pronouns are *she, they,* and *we.*
The correct sentences are:

She plays well.

They might win.

We are the winners.

Underline the correct pronouns that are thought completers
in the sentences below.

The ball hit I.   The ball hit me.

Vivian chased she.   Vivian chased her.

Greg gave us the ball.   Greg gave we the ball.

The correct thought completer pronouns are *me, her,* and *us.*
The correct sentences are:

The ball hit *me.*

Vivian chased *her.*

Greg gave *us* the ball.

Practice

Underline the correct pronoun for each sentence below.

1. (Me, I) help my neighbor.

2. (She, Her) is 85 years old.

3. Sometimes, (her, she) feels great.

4. At other times, I help (she, her) make dinner.

5. Mrs. Aberthy gives (me, I) presents.

6. One time, she gave (I, me) two bracelets.

7. (She, Her) bought (they, them) in Jamaica.

8. (Them, They) are beautiful.

9. My family often invites (her, she) to visit (we, us).

10. (We, Us) love her stories about her childhood.

Check your answers on page 117.

Follow-Up

Write five sentences about your family using pronouns, not the people's names. Circle the subject pronouns. Underline the pronouns that are thought completers. A sentence may have one, two, or three pronouns. Here's an example:

(He) cooks us breakfast.

Connectors

What You Know Suppose someone asks you who is going to a party tonight. Would you say something like the following?

> Jane is going to the party. Alex is going to the party. Fred is going to the party.

You probably wouldn't answer the question that way. It sounds silly to have so many short sentences. It would sound better to say:

> Jane, Alex, and Fred are going to the party.

In this sentence, words that belong together are connected.

How It Works

Sometimes you want to connect words or ideas that belong together or relate to each other in some way. When this happens, you use connectors. A **connector** is a word that connects or joins words, groups of words, or sentences.

In this lesson, you will learn about connectors that join words and groups of words. The two connectors used most often to do this are *and* and *or*.

The connector *and* is used to link closely related things or ideas together. For example:

> The chair *and* sofa are in the truck.

> Lorraine is carrying groceries, keys, *and* flowers.

> Manuel sings *and* plays the guitar.

In each of these sentences, the connector *and* links words that relate to each other.

Describe things that you see in this picture. Use connecting words to link related things.

The connector *or* is used to show a choice between two or more things. For example:

Victor *or* Olivia will take care of the baby.

Carrie will wear the red dress *or* the blue suit.

After work, I read *or* watch TV.

In each of these sentences, the connector *or* shows a choice.
Connectors can be used to link two or more subjects of a sentence.

The chair and sofa are in the truck.

Victor or Olivia will take care of the baby.

The *chair and sofa* are the subjects of the first sentence. *Victor or Olivia* is the subject of the second sentence.
Connectors can be used to link two or more thought completers.

Lorraine is carrying *groceries, keys, and flowers*.

Carrie will wear *the red dress or the blue suit*.

Connectors can also be used to link two or more verbs.

Manuel *sings and plays* the guitar.

After work, I *read or watch* TV.

Try It

Underline the connector in each sentence. On the answer blank, write *S* if the connector links the subjects, *TC* if the connector links the thought completers, or *V* if the connector links the verbs.

We can meet at a restaurant or my house. _____

The connector *or* links the thought completers *a restaurant* and *my house*. So the answer is TC.

Angelo, Pete, and Paula are coming with us. _____

The connector *and* links the subjects *Angelo*, *Pete*, and *Paula*. So the answer is *S*.

Practice

Underline the connector in each sentence. On the answer blank, write *S* if the connector links the subjects, *TC* if the connector links the thought completers, or *V* if the connector links the verbs.

1. Rita and Tomas are getting married this summer. _____

2. The wedding will be in a church or a large hall. _____

3. They are inviting friends and relatives. _____

4. Rita's sister designs and makes clothes. _____

5. She will make the bridal gown and the bridesmaids' dresses. _____

6. The bridesmaids are Wendy, Tanya, and Cara. _____

7. Rita's brother or Tomas's friend will be the best man. _____

8. There will be lots of singing and dancing. _____

Check your answers on page 117.

Follow-Up

There are many famous "pairs," such as salt and pepper, shoes and socks, and boys and girls. How many famous pairs can you think of?

What Is a Compound Sentence?

What You Know   Have you ever been late for a date? If so, you may have said something like this to your roommate as you grabbed your coat:

> I am going to the 9:00 show.

As you walked out the door, you may have called out:

> I will see you after midnight.

Perhaps if you hadn't been in such a hurry, you would have combined your thoughts into one sentence and said:

> I am going to the 9:00 show, so I will see you after midnight.

Combining ideas from two sentences into one sentence can make your thoughts clearer.

How It Works

You have learned that a sentence is a group of words that has a subject and a verb and expresses a complete thought. As long as it has one thought, it is one sentence. This kind of sentence is called a **simple sentence**. Both examples below are simple sentences:

> I am going to the 9:00 show.

> I will see you after midnight.

Sometimes your thoughts will be clearer and easier to understand if you combine two simple sentences into one sentence. This is called a **compound sentence**.

To make a compound sentence, you must use a connector. Before the connector, you must add a comma.

> I am going to the 9:00 show, <u>so</u> I will see you after midnight.

Look carefully at what is happening in this picture. Write a compound sentence telling two different things that are happening.

You learned about two connectors in Lesson 20—*and* and *or*. You may use these connectors to make compound sentences. Two other connectors are often used. They are *so* and *but*. The connector you use depends on the reason you want to combine the sentences.

The connector *and* is used to join two simple sentences that go together or relate to each other. For example:

You wash the dishes. I will clear off the table.

You wash the dishes, <u>and</u> I will clear off the table.

The two thoughts—washing dishes and clearing the table—relate to each other.

The connector *or* is used to show a choice or to show that there are different ways of doing something. For example:

You can drive. You can take a train.

You can drive, <u>or</u> you can take a train.

In this sentence, you are shown two different ways of doing something. You can choose one of them.

The connector *so* is used to show that one thing happened because of the other. For example:

I was late. You were angry with me.

I was late, <u>so</u> you were angry with me.

In this case, you were angry *because* I was late.

The connector *but* is used when one thought is the opposite of the other thought. It shows the contrast between the two thoughts. For example:

She wants to go to the fair tonight. I want to go to the movies tonight.

She wants to go to the fair tonight, but I want to go to the movies tonight.

Here, the thought of going to the fair is contrasted with the thought of going to the movies. It would not make sense to combine these sentences if the two people wanted to do the two things at different times. The thoughts are opposite because both people want to do both things at the same time.

Try It

Read the two simple sentences below. Then combine them into one sentence, using a comma and a connector. Write the compound sentence on the answer blank.

People crossed the street slowly. The driver honked his horn.

_____

The compound sentence should be:

People crossed the street slowly, *so* the driver honked his horn.

Did you use the connector *so*? It shows that the driver honked his horn because people walked slowly.
Now combine these two sentences into one.

I don't like horror movies. I will see this one anyway.

_____

The correct connector is *but*.

I don't like horror movies, *but* I will see this one anyway.

The *but* tells that there is a contrast between the two thoughts—not liking horror movies, on one hand, and going to see a horror movie, on the other hand.

Practice

Read the two simple sentences in each item below. Then combine them into one sentence, using a comma and a connector. Write the compound sentence on the answer blank.

1. Jeanette works in a bookstore on weekdays. She works in a restaurant on weekends.

   _____

2. She is very busy. She doesn't have much time to see her friends.

   _____

3. Jeanette likes to read about life in other countries. Her mother likes to read about history.

   _____

4. Her friend Denzel likes mystery books. She looks for mysteries when a new shipment of books arrives.

   _____

5. Jeanette would like to be the store manager. She would like to travel.

   _____

Check your answers on page 118.

Follow-Up

Here are some interesting facts. Make up a simple sentence and add it to each of these sentences to form a compound sentence. Compare your sentences with the ones made up by other people in the class.

1. Each zebra has its own pattern of stripes.

2. The highest temperature ever recorded was 136 degrees.

3. More men than women are color-blind.

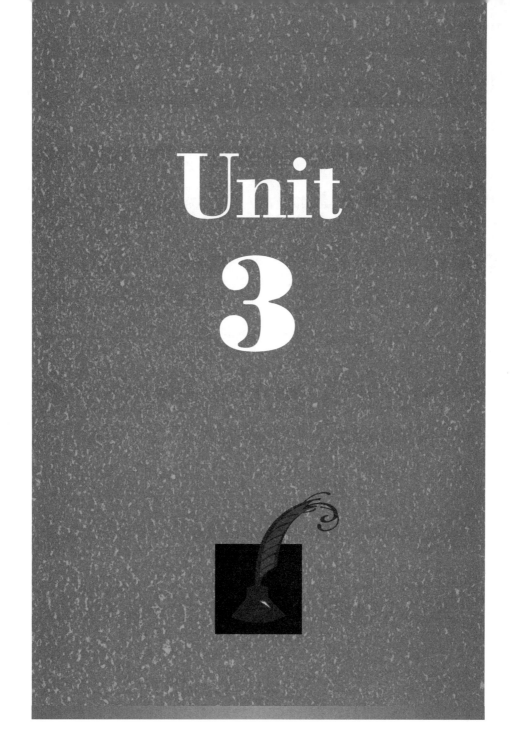

Unit 3

Paragraphs

Creating Paragraphs

What You Know Suppose you are thinking of taking a trip. You would like to visit Canada, so you decide to buy a guidebook. At the bookstore, there are two books on Canada. Below are the opening sentences from each book. Based on these two small samples, which book do you think you might buy?

Canada on 10 Canadian Dollars a Day

Canada is the second-largest country in the world. Australia, which is also a country, is a continent, too. Continents are very large land areas. In Canada, most people speak English. English is spoken in other places throughout the world. French is spoken in Quebec, Canada. French is spoken in France and in many other places.

Canada Today

If you're thinking of taking a vacation in Canada, you've picked the right country. There is so much to see and do. In western Canada, you can visit the Rocky Mountains and see bears and other wildlife. There are plenty of winter sports, such as skiing, ice skating, and ice hockey. Quebec City, where the official language is French, is the oldest city in Canada. If you're very adventurous, you might want to go to the northwest, to the Yukon Territory. Moose and beavers may greet you. It was here that gold rush fever took over in the 1890s.

Most people would choose the book called *Canada Today*. It gives useful information about Canada. The information is presented clearly and in a way that makes sense.

The book titled *Canada on 10 Canadian Dollars a Day* does not give information that might help a tourist who is visiting Canada. It jumps from one idea to the next. The sentences contain information about Australia, continents, English, and French. Few details are given about Canada.

How It Works

One way writers organize their thoughts is in paragraphs. A **paragraph** is a group of sentences about one main idea. The **main idea** is the thought or subject that all the sentences are about.

Paragraphs always begin on a new line. They are usually **indented**. This means that the first line begins farther to the right than the other lines.

In the example on page 68 from *Canada Today*, all the sentences include information that could help a person who wants to visit Canada. Since all the sentences are about one main idea, they make up a paragraph.

The sentences from *Canada on 10 Canadian Dollars a Day* include many details that do not relate to the main idea. This group of sentences is not a paragraph.

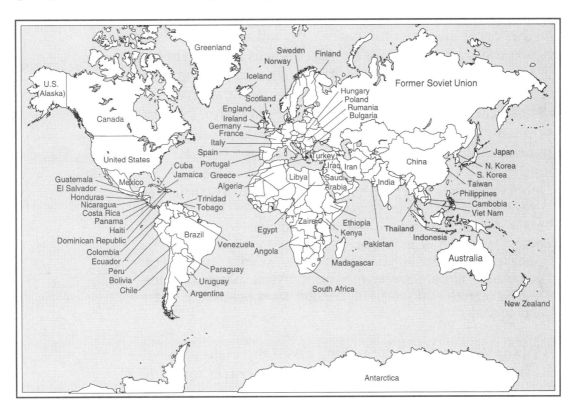

If you could visit any country in the world, which one would you choose? Why?

Try It

Read this group of sentences. Decide whether or not the sentences make up a paragraph.

> Africa is an interesting place to visit. The tallest mountain in Africa is Kilimanjaro. Mount Everest, however, is the world's tallest mountain. It is not in Africa, but lies between China and Nepal. The first people to reach the top of Mount Everest were Sir Edmund Hillary and Tenzing Norgay. The Sahara Desert is in Africa. Camels are good desert animals. You can see camels in zoos. Some zoos even have camel rides. The largest city in Africa is Cairo. My cousin once rode a camel.

Not all the sentences relate to the main idea—*Africa is an interesting place to visit.* One sentence tells about Mount Everest, which is not in Africa. Another tells who the first people were to reach the top of Everest. Other sentences tell about camels, zoos, and even the writer's cousin. These sentences are not about the main idea. The main idea is that Africa is an interesting place to visit. Therefore, this group of sentences is not a paragraph.

Here is another group of sentences about visiting Africa. As you read the sentences, see if all the sentences relate to the main idea.

> Africa is an interesting place to visit. There are over 50 countries to see. Cairo, the capital of the country of Egypt, is the largest city in Africa. Kilimanjaro is the tallest mountain in Africa, rising over 19,000 feet. It is located in the country of Tanzania. The Sahara Desert, the largest desert in the world, covers almost one third of Africa. Deserts, mountains, rivers, valleys, swamps, and plains make up Africa's landscape. Most people live in the countryside.

All the sentences tell something about the main idea— *Africa is an interesting place to visit.* So, the sentences make up a paragraph.

Practice

The group of sentences on page 71 contains three sentences that do not relate to the main idea. Write the sentences that do *not* relate to the main idea on the blank lines.

Can you find what does not belong in this picture? In a similar way, when you are writing you look for sentences that do not belong in a paragraph.

Being a travel agent isn't easy. People call and ask me to suggest a place to visit. If a person wants to visit a cold place, I might suggest Canada or Alaska. I have a horrible cold today. If someone would like to visit a place that is hot, I might suggest Mexico, South America, or even Florida or California. My mother lives in Florida. Some people want to stay close to home. For these people, I might suggest going to a hotel near the water or to a hotel in the mountains. Sharks are always a danger in the waters.

1. _____

2. _____

3. _____

Check your answers on page 118.

Follow-Up

The first sentence of three different paragraphs is shown below. Each sentence tells the main idea of a paragraph. Choose one of the sentences and finish writing the paragraph.

1. On my last vacation, nothing went right.

2. The job I would most like to have is _____.

3. People from all over the world come to the United States to live.

Topic Sentences

What You Know   Have you ever written a letter asking for a job interview? Pretend that you are the person who wants to hire someone. You receive a letter. The first paragraph is shown below.

> I have three years experience in a position at the Howe Company. On that job, I greeted visitors, answered phones, and took messages. I also have done some typing on an IBM personal computer with WordPerfect for Windows software.

Is something missing from this paragraph? If you said that there is no sentence that clearly states what the paragraph is about, you would be right. It would have been better to begin the paragraph with a sentence something like this:

> I am applying for the job of receptionist.

How It Works

A **topic sentence** states the main idea of a paragraph. All the other sentences in the paragraph relate to the topic sentence.

Topic sentences are important for two reasons:

1. Topic sentences tell the reader what is coming.

2. Topic sentences help the writer focus his or her thoughts. Writers try to make sure that all their sentences give information about the main idea.

In the example above, the topic sentence is: *I am applying for the job of receptionist.* All the other sentences give information about this main idea.

In silent films, moviegoers could not hear what the actors said. Except for some "titles," their actions alone told all of the story.

Usually, a topic sentence comes at the beginning of a paragraph. However, sometimes a topic sentence can come in the middle or at the end of a paragraph. Here are two examples:

The first films were silent. What the actors said was printed in words at the bottom of the screen. These words were called *titles*. The titles explained what was going on. A piano player worked in the theater. He played the kind of music that seemed to go with the scene in the movie. The first full-length "talkie" was shown in 1927. It had sound. Today, films have fabulous special effects. People can fly through the air or crash through layers of earth. Films have come a long way since their beginning in 1895.

The topic sentence of this paragraph is the last sentence—*Films have come a long way since their beginning in 1895*. Each sentence in the paragraph gives information about the changes in films over the years.

Here's another paragraph. Can you find the topic sentence?

If there are outlaws, gangs, and tough guys in the movie, I can't take my eyes off the screen. If a person is being followed night and day, I'm on the edge of my seat. A movie about "normal" people who turn out to be crazy gives me goose bumps. I love all suspense movies. If there's a murder, I'm thrilled. *Psycho* is one of my all-time favorites. Another movie I love is *Rear Window*.

The topic sentence in this paragraph is *I love all suspense movies*. All the other sentences give information about the main idea.

If you were to write a paragraph describing what is taking place in this photograph from the movie *North by Northwest*, what might your topic sentence be?

Try It

There is a topic sentence in the paragraph below. Can you find it? When you do, underline it.

Alfred Hitchcock had a long and successful career as a filmmaker. *The Pleasure Garden* was the first film he directed, in 1925. However, he considered *The Lodger* his first true film. *The Lodger*, directed by Hitchcock in 1926, is about a landlady who thinks that her tenant is Jack the Ripper, who was a famous murderer in the late 1800s. *The Man Who Knew Too Much* is considered by many people to be the first movie in which Hitchcock showed his skill at making suspense films. After that film came other suspenseful films. Among the most famous are *The Thirty-Nine Steps*, *The Lady Vanishes*, *Lifeboat*, *Rear Window*, *Vertigo*, *North by Northwest*, and *Psycho*.

The topic sentence is the first sentence: *Alfred Hitchcock had a long and successful career as a filmmaker*. All the other sentences in the paragraph give information about his career as a filmmaker.

Practice

Read the paragraphs below. Decide which sentence in each paragraph is the topic sentence. Underline each topic sentence.

1. I arrive at the theater each evening at 5 P.M. As soon as I take off my coat, I go directly to the refreshment stand. It's my job to sell drinks, candy, and popcorn until 11 P.M. The most popular item is popcorn. The most popular drink is Coke. Working at a refreshment stand is my summer job.

2. Mickey Mouse is probably the most famous cartoon character in the world. Walt Disney first created him in 1928. Mickey was named Mortimer at first. The first film Mickey appeared in was called *Steamboat Willie*. Mickey's girlfriend Minnie and his dog Pluto became popular too, along with Pegleg Pete. Mickey became the main attraction on the TV show "The Mickey Mouse Club."

3. In the film *High Noon*, Gary Cooper plays a lawman. He fights alone for law and order in in a small western town that is filled with fear. *High Noon* is considered one of the best films about the West. The film takes place between 10:40 A.M. and noon. This is the same amount of time as the actual running time of the movie.

Check your answers on page 118.

Follow-Up

Look in one of your schoolbooks or a book you have at home. Read one or more paragraphs carefully. See whether you can find the topic sentence in each.

Supporting Sentences

What You Know
If you are like many people, you take the time to put your closets and drawers in order. Perhaps you have all your T-shirts in one drawer, your socks in another, and your sweaters in a third. Maybe you have all your shirts or blouses hanging next to each other in the closet, and all your pants or slacks in a group hanging next to them.

If you are like many people, you may also have one drawer that seems to have a little bit of everything in it—some jewelry, maybe a belt or two, an old wallet, several scarves, and a few old photographs.

When you're in a hurry and you're looking for something, which drawer would you rather look in—one of your neat drawers or your "everything" drawer?

How It Works
Sentences in a paragraph can be compared to clothing in a drawer or closet. The meaning of sentences in a paragraph can be grasped most easily when they are organized.

The most important sentence in a paragraph is the topic sentence. All the other sentences support, or help, the topic sentence. These other sentences have the details that help explain the topic. They are called **supporting sentences** or **supporting details**.

The supporting details in a paragraph can be arranged in several different ways: **time order**, **order of importance**, and **spatial** (SPAY-shuhl) **order**. (Spatial order means an organization based on where things are placed.)

When sentences are arranged in *time order*, the events are told in the order in which they happen—the first event first, the next event second, and the third event third. Here's a short example of sentences arranged in time order:

> When you walk your dog, here's what you should do. First, offer him a biscuit so that he comes to you. Then, take his leash off the door knob. Command him to sit. Put on his leash. Tell him to heel.

Writers arrange sentences in *order of importance* when they are trying to convince someone of something. Writers might put their strongest point first, or they might save it for last. Here's an example, with the most important point coming first. Notice that the first sentence is a topic sentence. It tells the main idea of the paragraph.

Restaurants should ban cigarette smoking completely. First, cigarette smoking is a proven killer. In addition, when people are eating, they usually don't like the smell of cigarette smoke. It gets in their faces and in their hair. Finally, it is sometimes annoying for nonsmokers to watch smokers.

After the topic sentence, *Restaurants should ban cigarette smoking completely*, the most important point is given: Cigarette smoking is a proven killer. The second most important point is that many people dislike the smell of smoke while eating because it gets in their faces and their hair. The last sentence states the least important point.

Arranging sentences in *spatial order* helps when you want to write a description of how things look or where things are. Here's an example:

To the right of the front door of his apartment is the kitchen. It has a stove, sink, and refrigerator, but it is not big enough for a table or chairs. Straight ahead of the front door is the living room, which is long and narrow. A dining table and two chairs are in this room. They are near the kitchen. Tall open shelves separate the eating area from the living area.

This description of someone's apartment gives details about where things are and how big they are in relation to other things. Using spatial order helps readers see things in the way the writer sees them. It helps them get a picture in their mind of what something looks like.

Try It

Read the following paragraph. In what order are the details arranged? Is it time order, order of importance, or spatial order?

Two hundred years ago, the United States was a new nation. Throughout the 1800s, people moved west and settled the land. By 1900 the United States had many farms and factories. Today, the country is the most powerful one on earth.

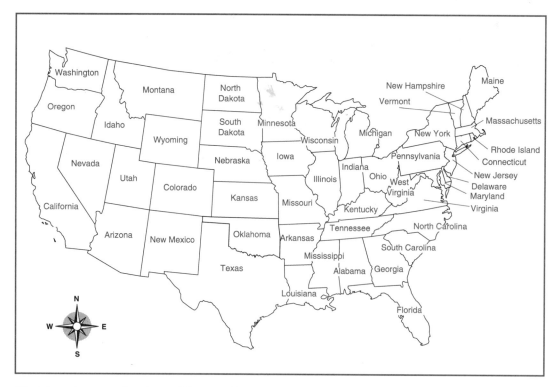

Find the state you live in on this map. Describe where it is located by using spatial order to give the details.

If you said that the details are arranged in time order, you'd be right. The first sentence tells what happened in the 1700s. The next sentence gives details about the 1800s. The third sentence tells about 1900, and the final sentence tells about today.

By arranging the sentences in the order in which the events happen, a writer does not confuse a reader. The paragraph would be confusing if it were not presented in time order.

Here's another paragraph. How are the details presented—in time order, spatial order, or order of importance?

> My grandparents live in Kansas. Kansas is in the center of the United States. To the south is Oklahoma. To the east is Missouri. North of Kansas is Nebraska. To the west is Colorado. Kansas is far from any ocean.

The details in the paragraph are arranged in spatial order. The location of Kansas is presented in relation to other states.

Practice

Each of the following paragraphs is arranged in one of these ways: *time order*, *order of importance*, or *spatial order*. Read each paragraph. Then, on the blank line, write the order in which the details are arranged.

1. When you go to Washington, D.C., there are certain things you must see. You have to go to the White House. There is no other place like it in the country. The Lincoln Memorial and the Washington Monument are also interesting to see. If you can find time, a trip to some museums is worthwhile.

   _____

2. When we arrived in Washington, D.C., we went directly to our hotel. Next, we unpacked, looked at some maps, and put on some comfortable shoes. Then we got on a sightseeing bus that took us all over the city. Our last stop was back at the hotel, 3 hours later.

   _____

3. Washington, D.C., is not easy to find on a map. It's in the eastern part of the country, north of Richmond, Virginia, and south of Annapolis, Maryland. It's west of Dover, Delaware.

   _____

Check your answers on page 118.

Follow-Up

Think of what's happened to you so far today. Write five separate sentences giving details. First, number the sentences in *time order*, telling which of the details occurred first, second, and so on. Then, rewrite the sentences. This time, number them in the *order of importance* to you, putting the number 1 next to the event that was most important, and the number 5 next to the least important event.

Telling a Story

What You Know   You may not realize it, but you tell stories every day. For example, you might tell a classmate what happened to you on your way to school. That's a story. You might tell a person something that took place between you and your boss. That's a story, too. At night, you might tell a story to a child before bedtime. Although this story may not be a true one, it is still a story.

How It Works

All stories, whether they are true or made-up, have several things in common: a plot, one or more characters, and a setting.

Every good story has a **plot**. A plot is what happens. It tells about the events that take place. Usually, the events are in time order.

Suppose you are listening to this story. Read it and see if it makes sense to you.

> On the way there, we got a flat tire. At last, the day came when Emma was to arrive. Lucky for us, the plane was 3 hours late! We got to the airport 2 hours late. We got up early and left for the airport at 5 A.M. Changing the tire was not easy. When Emma got off the plane, we recognized her right away.

You probably were confused after reading the story. The events were not presented in time order. Here is how the story should have been told.

> At last, the day came when Emma was to arrive. We got up early and left for the airport at 5 A.M. On the way there, we got a flat tire. Changing the tire was not easy. We got to the airport 2 hours late. Lucky for us, the plane was 3 hours late! When Emma got off the plane, we recognized her right away.

Here, the events are presented in the order in which they happened. They are also presented in a way that makes it clear to the reader what has happened and why.

A good story has interesting characters. **Characters** are the people in a story. Which character is more interesting—the one in the first paragraph below or the one in the second?

The woman was nice. She dressed in an interesting way. She was kind and pleasant. Everyone liked her a lot.

Mabel called everyone she met "darling." She always wore purple. On her tall, thin body, she wore purple dresses, purple coats, and purple shoes.

You probably thought that Mabel was more interesting. That's because you found out her name and something about her.

Using nouns and verbs that fit the characters helps make the characters seem real. Using adjectives and adverbs makes the characters really come alive.

A good story has a clear setting. The **setting** is where the story takes place. Using nouns and verbs that fit in with the setting helps make the place seem real. Using adjectives and adverbs can "paint a picture" with words of the setting.

Read these two descriptions of settings. Which is clearer?

I looked out the window and saw a beautiful scene. There were trees, a lake, and tall grass.

I looked out the window and saw a beautiful scene. The ground was covered with tall, thick grass that swayed in the wind. The lake was dark and quiet. The trees were full with fresh, green leaves. I could hear them rustle as the wind blew.

The second paragraph is clearer. It has nouns, verbs, adjectives, and adverbs that tell you how the setting looked and sounded.

Both these photos are of a living room. Which one would you rather visit?

Try It

Two descriptions are given here. Put a check mark next to the one that is clearer:

I was all dressed up. My dress was beautiful. I loved wearing it.

I was so nervous that you would think I was getting married instead of Nellie, my closest friend. I was her bridesmaid. I was wearing a peach silk dress with thin straps and a low neckline. The dress was tight at my waist and then fell softly to my ankles.

If you picked the second description, you are right. It gives specific details that let you know some things about the character. It also gives details so that you can almost see what is described.

Here are several events from the day of the wedding. Put a check mark next to the paragraph in which the details are presented in time order.

I looked for Garfield. He was not in the house, so I went outside and called him. Sometimes he hides under the porch. When he didn't come out from under the porch, I started walking down the street.

Sometimes he likes to hide under the porch. He was not in the house, so I went outside and called him. I looked for Garfield. When he didn't come out from under the porch, I started walking down the street.

The events in the first paragraph are in time order. The details are presented in the order in which they took place.

Here are two descriptions of a setting. Put a check mark next to the one you think is clearer.

The wedding was held in a big room.

The wedding was held in an enormous room in Rossini's Restaurant. There were 50 tables. The dishes and napkins on the tables were pink and purple. Each table had a vase of purple flowers.

The second description gives a clearer picture of the room.

Remember, to be a good storyteller, you should give details that make the characters, events, and setting come alive.

Practice 1

Here are some events that could be a part of a story. They are not in time order. Look them over. Then rewrite them in the order in which they probably took place.

1. After we were hot enough, we raced into the water.

2. We lay in the sun until we were very hot.

3. We dried off and ate a delicious picnic lunch.

1. _____

2. _____

3. _____

Practice 2

Here are the names of four characters. Write five sentences about each one, telling what this person might look like, act like, or wear.

Forgetful Fred   Energetic Edna

Lazy Lola   Nervous Ned

Practice 3

Choose one setting from the list below and write five sentences about it. Include sounds, smells, and sights.

1. an outdoor music concert   **3.** a dark alley

2. an empty park   **4.** a beach

Check your answers on page 119.

Follow-Up

Pick one character from Practice 2 and one setting from Practice 3 above. Put the character in the setting. Then choose one of these events to write a short story about:

An accident   A murder   A wedding

Lesson

26

Explaining How to Do Something

What You Know Has anyone ever tried to explain to you how to play a card game? Was the explanation clear? Did you get all the information you needed? Were the details presented in the correct order?

How It Works

When you want to explain how to do something, it's important to put the details in *time order*. If a detail is missing or is out of order, the explanation will be confusing.

One way to avoid confusion is to write down all the ideas you want to present. Then, number the details in the order in which they should appear. The following words can help make it easy to understand details presented in time order.

first	next	after	then
second	later	last	finally

Suppose you work in an office and are asked to explain to a new employee how to send a fax (a copy that is sent on the phone lines). Here are several details that you might want to include. Do you think they are in the best order?

1. Hang up. The machine will start sending the fax.

2. Pick up the telephone receiver and wait for the dial tone.

3. Place the pages to be sent face down in the slot and wait until you hear a beep.

4. Dial the number of the person you are sending the fax to.

5. When you hear a tone, press the start button.

84

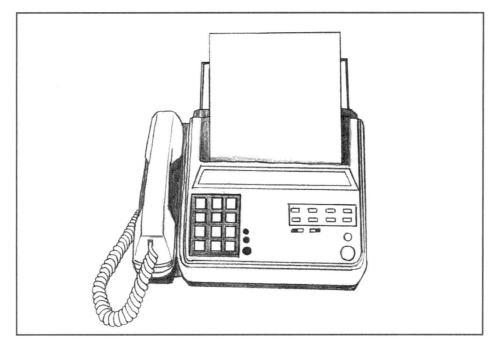

Sending a fax is easier than you might think.

How would you rearrange the details so that they are in time order? Look at this order:

1. Place the pages to be sent face down in the slot and wait until you hear a beep.

2. Pick up the telephone receiver and wait for the dial tone.

3. Dial the number of the person you are sending the fax to.

4. When you hear a tone, press the start button.

5. Hang up. The machine will start sending the fax.

If you were to write a paragraph explaining how to send a fax, you might write it this way:

First, place the pages to be sent face down in the slot and wait until you hear a beep. Then, pick up the telephone receiver and wait for the dial tone. Next, dial the number of the person you are sending the fax to. When you hear a tone, press the start button. Last, hang up. The machine will start sending the fax.

The words *first, then, next,* and *last* help make a clearer picture of exactly how to send a fax.

Try It

Here's a paragraph that explains how to bake cookies. The sentences are out of order. Read the paragraph carefully. Then rewrite it on the answer blanks so that the sentences are in the right order. (Hint: Read all the sentences first. Number each one lightly in pencil to help you rewrite the paragraph.)

Baking cookies is fun. Mix all the ingredients together. Take them out of the oven and let them cool on a rack for 5 minutes. Preheat the oven to 350 degrees. You will need eggs, milk, flour, chocolate chips, and butter. After you serve them, everyone will beg for more! Bake the cookies in the oven for 10 minutes. Put the cookie dough on a cookie sheet. Separate the eggs. Melt the butter.

_____

_____

_____

_____

_____

_____

_____

Here is the paragraph rewritten in correct order.

Baking cookies is fun. You will need eggs, milk, flour, chocolate chips, and butter. Preheat the oven to 350 degrees. Separate the eggs. Melt the butter. Mix all the ingredients together. Put the cookie dough on a cookie sheet. Bake the cookies in the oven for 10 minutes. Take them out of the oven and let them cool on a rack for 5 minutes.

This paragraph now makes sense. The information is in time order. However, are all the details included that explain how to bake cookies? What is missing? You need to know: how much flour, milk, and butter, and how many eggs and chocolate chips to use, how to form the cookies, how much cookie dough to use for each cookie. In addition, you need to know the order in which to mix the ingredients.

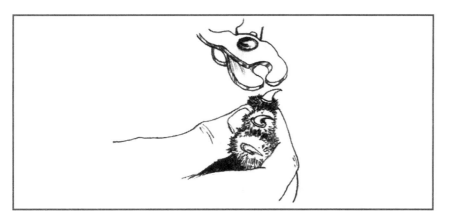

This shows how to hold a cat's paw when you clip its front claws.

Practice

Here's a paragraph that explains how to clip a cat's front claws. The sentences are out of order. Rewrite the paragraph on a blank sheet of paper so that the sentences are in the right order. Remember to read all the sentences first. You may number them lightly with a pencil to help you rewrite the paragraph.

Your finger should be on the bottom of the toe, and your thumb should be on the top. Lift one of the front legs. Get special nail clippers from a pet store. Then do the same thing to the claws on the other paw. Clip all the claws on one paw. Hold the cat on your lap or put the cat on a table in front of you. Hold the cat's toe with your thumb and forefinger. Clip the tip of the claw just where it begins to curve downward. Be sure not to clip the pink area of the claw, because this will cause bleeding. When you press your finger and thumb together, the claw will move outward.

Check your answers on page 119.

Follow-Up

Is there something you know how to do well? Write several sentences telling how to do it. Once you have all the details, put the sentences in the correct order. Ask a friend to read them. Ask your friend whether the sentences are clear.

Telling Your Opinion

What You Know If you've ever had a discussion about something you feel very strongly about, you know what can happen. You can get very emotional. Your ideas can become confused. You might start yelling. You might get so excited that you can't think clearly.

Stating your opinion in a clear, logical way can be difficult, but it's not impossible. If you can do it, you might be able to convince someone else to see things your way!

How It Works

It is important to understand the difference between fact and opinion. A **fact** is something that can be proven as real or true. For example, your age and your address are facts.

An **opinion** states a belief, value, or choice. Even though your age is a fact, whether you are young or old can be an opinion. (Ask someone 7 years old and someone 70 years old whether you are young or old.)

When you express an opinion, begin with a topic sentence. Then, be sure to include as many reasons as you can think of to support your opinion. Facts make stronger arguments than emotions.

Read these two paragraphs. They both have the same topic sentence. Which one is better?

Cigarette smoking should not be allowed in public places. People who smoke are crazy and selfish. They are stupid, too. I hate all people who smoke. If you smoke, you're an idiot. I just can't believe people are so dumb.

Cigarette smoking should not be allowed in public places. Studies show that second-hand smoke can kill. Why should nonsmokers be forced to breathe in other people's smoke? Smoke causes people's eyes to burn. Some people find it difficult to breathe when there is cigarette smoke in the air. There is no excuse for allowing cigarette smokers to make others breathe bad air.

Many cities have laws that ban smoking in some or all public places. What is your opinion on this?

If you think that the second paragraph is stronger, you're right. Many reasons are given to support the main idea. The ideas are presented calmly. Most of the ideas are facts.

The speaker in the first paragraph expresses his or her opinion without any facts. Few details support the opinion. The speaker does not seem to have thought a great deal about the subject.

Here is another way to help you make a strong case for your opinion. State ideas that appeal to a person's feelings. For example, if you want to convince someone not to smoke, you might say something like this:

You know, you may not be around to see your child grow up if you smoke.

Although the idea is not a fact, it could help make a person see things differently.

Both facts and emotions are important in expressing an opinion. Facts show that you know what you are talking about. Appealing to someone's emotions makes your argument strong. However, expressing an opinion based only on emotions may cause arguments and bad feelings.

Try It

Suppose you've been asked to be on a committee to decide whether to spend money to improve the grounds outside your apartment building. The meeting at which the committee members will express their opinions will take place tonight. In order to prepare, you decide to write down some of your ideas. Here is what you write. Underline the ideas that you think people might listen to seriously at the meeting.

1. This building is awful.

2. Some tenants might plant flowers, and others can be in charge of watering them.

3. We could make a small park on the west side of the building.

4. If we improve the way our building looks, we will all feel better about living here.

5. Kids are always playing their radios so loud that I can't think.

6. We might put benches around the south side of the building.

7. We have $500 to make improvements. Buying a few trees and planting some flowers is within our budget.

8. Kids need a place to play, and older people need places to sit.

9. Committees are stupid!

If you answered that the numbers 2, 3, 4, 6, 7, and 8 express ideas that people might listen to seriously, you're right. They express facts or appeal to people's feelings. Items 1, 5, and 9 show strong emotions, but they do not present ideas about the specific topic—improving the grounds outside your apartment building.

The people in this picture are expressing their opinions by protesting.

Practice

Here is one person's opinion about why school should be open 12 months a year. Underline the sentences that you feel *do not belong* in a paragraph expressing an opinion on this subject.

School should be open 12 months a year. Students in the United States are not doing as well as students in other countries on many tests. Students in Japan, for example, go to school throughout the year. The Japanese score better than Americans do on most tests. Most kids hate school, but who cares. The only way that we can compete successfully in business with the rest of the world is to have students who are as skilled as students from other countries. In some countries, kids don't even go to school at all, so look how lucky we are. The best way to compete with other countries is to offer more schooling to our citizens. A 12-month school year is the answer.

Check your answers on page 119.

Follow-Up

Write a paragraph in which you express an opinion on something you feel very strongly about, such as owning handguns or the legal drinking age. Do some research so that you will have some facts to include. Write down all your ideas. Then, put the ideas in the order in which you want to express them. Begin with a topic sentence that clearly states your opinion.

Revising Paragraphs

What You Know Latisha Williams wants to work as a helper in a children's zoo. She was asked to write a paragraph telling why she should get the job.

> I have two dogs and a cat of my own. I have been baby-sitting for several years, and I have two younger brothers. Their names are Arthur and Aaron. Working in the Children's Zoo will give me valuable experience toward my goal of becoming a worker in an animal hospital. I love both animals and children. My favorite subject in school is math. I also worked in Pete's Pet Shop, where I fed, brushed, bathed, and took care of 40 animals.

There are no spelling or grammar mistakes in this paragraph. However, there are some things that could be improved.

How It Works

You have learned to plan what you write. However, once you have written something, you must check it carefully to make sure that you have expressed your thoughts in the best possible way.

What you write first is called a **first draft** or a **rough draft**. Most writers have to fix what they write. This is called **revising**.

Whenever you write a first draft of a paragraph, look over your work. Here is the checklist of questions to ask yourself:

1. Is there a topic sentence?

2. Does the topic sentence clearly state the main idea?

3. Is the topic sentence in the best place in the paragraph?

4. Do details, facts, and reasons support the main idea?

5. Is the information arranged in the most logical order: time order, spatial order, order of importance?

6. Does the paragraph have any information that is not related to the topic sentence?

This is a picture of Toni Morrison, a great American writer. She, along with everyone who writes, has to revise her writing.

Look back at the paragraph Latisha wrote about the zoo. If you had written the paragraph, here's what you should do to revise it.

Refer to the first question on the checklist: Is there a topic sentence? No. Here is a possible topic sentence:

I am applying for the job of helper at the Children's Zoo.

Does this topic sentence clearly state the main idea? Yes. Where in the paragraph would be the best place for this topic sentence? The best place would be at the beginning, so that the reader will know right away what the paragraph is about.

The fourth question on the checklist is about details, facts, and reasons. The paragraph does include this kind of information.

The next question is about the order of the information. Is it logical? No. The best kind of order for this paragraph would be order of importance. First, you should give the most important reason why you think that you should get the job.

The last question asks whether the paragraph has information that should not be there. The brothers' names and the favorite school subject don't belong in the paragraph.

Here is how the paragraph could be revised.

I am applying for the job of helper at the Children's Zoo. I love both animals and children. I have two dogs and a cat of my own. I worked in Pete's Pet Shop, where I fed, brushed, bathed, and took care of 40 animals. I have been baby-sitting for several years. Working in the Children's Zoo will give me valuable experience toward my goal of becoming a worker at an animal hospital.

Try It

When you revise a paragraph you have written, first make sure that you have a topic sentence and that it is the best one possible.

Suppose you need to write a paragraph that explains the job at the Children's Zoo. Which of the following sentences would be the best topic sentence for it? Underline your answer.

Feeding the animals is one part of the job.

Your day begins at 9 A.M.

The job of helper at the Children's Zoo involves feeding animals and taking children on tours.

The third sentence is the best topic sentence. It clearly states what the paragraph will be about. The other two sentences do not cover all the ideas that will appear in the paragraph.

Suppose you are asked to write a paragraph about the history of the Children's Zoo. Here are three possible topic sentences for it. Underline the one you think is best.

The Children's Zoo is a fun place.

The Children's Zoo, located on Stanton Street, has been pleasing both children and animals since 1985.

Today, the Children's Zoo costs $4 for an adult to visit and 50 cents for a child to visit.

Only the second sentence covers all the information you would write about in a history of the zoo.

Imagine that you are writing paragraphs on the three subjects below. How would you arrange the information within each paragraph: in time order, in spatial order, or in order of importance?

Where to Find the Bears _____

You would arrange the information here in *spatial order*, telling where in the zoo the bears are located in relation to other animals.

How to Feed a Bear _____

Here the information should be arranged in *time order*, telling the order in which to do things.

Why Bears Are Valuable Animals _____

This information should be arranged in *order of importance*.

A modern zoo.

Practice 1

Here are three possible topic sentences. Pick the one that you think would be best in a paragraph about modern zoos.

In many zoos today, animals roam freely over large land areas that have trees and grass and other wildlife.

A few zoos don't treat their animals kindly.

Visit a zoo and enjoy a picnic on the grounds.

Practice 2

Decide how the information in a paragraph on each of these topics should be presented. Write *time order*, *spatial order*, or *order of importance* on each answer blank.

1. Why zoos should not keep their animals in small pens. _____

2. How to find the information booth. _____

3. How to clean the rabbit pen. _____

Check your answers on page 119.

Follow-Up

Write a short paragraph on one of the following topics. Use the checklist on page 92 to revise your work. (1) It's important for every citizen to vote. (2) My first home. (3) My best day.

Editing Paragraphs

What You Know   Imagine that your daughter wants to go to camp more than anything. You call the director of the camp. She tells you that all 50 places are already taken. You ask whether she could fit in one more child. After a long silence, the camp director tells you to write a note about your daughter. She just might let in one more child.

Here's what you write. Do you think Carlota's chances of going to camp are good or not?

> Carlota is a wonderful child. She love all sports, especially basketball. She and I plays every evening. She win almost always! Carlota enjoyed reading, taking long walks, and dancing. She is a great dancer. Gets excellent grades in school. Does careful work.

How It Works

After you write the first draft of a paragraph, there are several things you should check for when reading it over. In Lesson 28, a checklist for revising paragraphs was given. In this lesson, you are asked to look for mistakes in subject–verb agreement and in verb tense. This kind of checking is often called **editing**.

Look back at the paragraph about Carlota. There are three mistakes in subject–verb agreement. Can you find them?

As you learned in Lesson 18, subjects and verbs must agree in number. Here are two mistakes in agreement from the paragraph:

> She love all sports, especially basketball.

> She win almost always!

In both sentences, the subject, *she,* is singular but the verbs *love* and *win* are plural. Here are the two sentences written correctly.

> She loves all sports, especially basketball.

> She wins almost always!

The people in this picture work as editors. They check grammar, spelling, and other matters in things that writers have written.

In another sentence from the paragraph, the subject—*she and I*—is plural but the verb—*plays*—is singular.

She and I plays every evening.

This is how the sentence should be written:

She and I play every evening.

In the paragraph about Carlota, there is one mistake in verb tense. Can you find it?

The verb *enjoyed* is in the past tense. It should be in the present tense like all the other verbs in the paragraph. This is how the sentence should be written:

Carlota enjoys reading, taking long walks, and dancing.

There are two sentences in the paragraph that are not complete. In Lesson 16, you learned that every sentence must have a subject and verb in order to be complete.

Here are two groups of words from the paragraph that do not have subjects. Can you correct them?

Gets excellent grades in school.

Does careful work.

Here are these two sentences with subjects:

Carlota gets excellent grades in school.

She does careful work.

Try It

Each of these sentences has a mistake in subject–verb agreement. Underline the mistake in each sentence.

> Harry live in Georgia.
>
> His parents loves living there.

In the first sentence, the singular subject, *Harry*, is followed by a plural verb, *live*. The sentence should be written this way:

> Harry lives in Georgia.

In the second sentence, the plural subject, *parents*, is followed by a singular verb, *loves*. The sentence should be written this way:

> His parents love living here.

In the following paragraph, one group of words is not a complete sentence. Underline this group of words.

> Harry and his brother plant fruits and vegetables. Enjoy working in the garden. All the members of the family eat the tomatoes, lettuce, and peaches that they grow.

The group of words that is not a sentence is *enjoy working in the garden*. This group of words is missing a subject. Here is how the words might be written:

> They enjoy working in the garden.

In the following sentences, there is one mistake in verb tense. Underline the mistake.

> Each evening, we eat dinner in the kitchen. Everyone talked at once. We always have fun.

The verb *talked* is in the past tense. It should be in the present tense. The sentence should be written this way:

> Everyone talks at once.

Practice

Here is a paragraph that has two mistakes in subject–verb agreement, two verbs that are not in the correct tense, and two groups of words that are not sentences. Read the paragraph. Then, rewrite it carefully on the answer blanks. Correct all the errors.

Jed is my best friend. Moving to Florida. Jed want to move. Loves warm weather. He liked to water ski. He and his brother loves to swim. Jed enjoyed playing tennis. Miss him.

_____

_____

_____

_____

_____

Check your answers on page 119.

Follow-Up

Now that you have come to the last lesson of the book, you should congratulate yourself. You have done a lot of work and learned a great deal.

For your last assignment, look over a paragraph you have written recently and check for mistakes in subject–verb agreement and in verb tense. Make sure that all your sentences are related to the main idea and that your topic sentence clearly states the main idea.

Congratulations!

Unit Reviews

Unit 1 Review
Lesson 1

Add words to each group of words below so that the words make sense.

1. _____ is my favorite holiday.

2. We went to the _____.

3. The movie was _____.

4. _____ pays the rent.

5. _____ in the evening.

6. _____ went to _____.

7. The dog _____.

8. Winter _____.

9. Ben lives in _____.

10. Jill hopes to _____.

Lesson 2

Underline the singular nouns in these sentences.

1. A squirrel likes to gather nuts.

2. A bird eats worms.

3. The cat drinks the milk.

4. Turtles live longer than any other creature on earth.

5. A turtle has a shell.

6. The blue whale is the largest animal in the world.

7. Usually, a wolf will not attack a person.

8. A cow eats grass and hay.

9. A spider spins a web.

10. The mouse runs along the wall.

Lesson 3

Underline the plural nouns in these sentences.

1. Some birds build nests out of twigs.

2. Camels do not store water in their humps.

3. Some sharks will eat almost anything.

4. There are more insects in the world than any other kind of animal.

5. The trunk of an elephant has no bones.

6. Lions hunt zebras.

7. Bees make honey.

8. Some dogs look like wolves.

9. Clams have shells.

10. Snakes can kill elephants.

Lesson 4

Underline the pronouns in each sentence.

1. I gave her a kiss.

2. She gave me a hug.

3. We went to visit him.

4. Les went with us.

5. We saw our cousin.

6. He is staying with them.

7. The family gave him a gift.

8. They want us to see her.

9. We left our car near you.

10. It belongs to her.

Lesson 5

Underline the adjectives—including articles—in each sentence.

1. Jimmy bought a red car.

2. The new car has leather seats.

3. Five people can fit in the car.

4. Jimmy took two friends for a long ride.

5. They drove by the large lake near the woods.

6. They passed the old schoolhouse.

7. Jimmy showed them the new park.

8. Tammy wanted to visit Lynn in the next town.

9. Otto hoped to see the football stadium.

10. The day was a great success.

Lesson 6

Underline the verb in each sentence.

1. Roberta bought food for dinner.

2. She carried it home.

3. Eli chopped the onions.

4. Sam peeled carrots.

5. Roberta boiled some water.

6. Eli washed the lettuce.

7. He cut the tomatoes.

8. Sam placed dishes on the table.

9. Eli put the spaghetti in the water.

10. Roberta served the dinner.

Lesson 7

Underline the adverb in each sentence.

1. Bob jogs slowly.

2. Cerise plays tennis gracefully.

3. Karen swims fast.

4. I walk quickly.

5. Some people exercise gladly.

6. Maria skates carefully.

7. Andrew dives beautifully.

8. Marty skates proudly.

9. Some people exercise often.

10. Others never exercise.

Lesson 8

Underline the adverb or adverbs in each sentence.

1. Giselle works very carefully.

2. Jimmy works more quickly than Giselle.

3. Jimmy is fairly careless.

4. Giselle makes almost no mistakes.

5. The boss wants employees who work fast, but not so fast that they make mistakes.

6. She would like to find an employee who works really fast and extremely accurately.

7. She thought she would never find such a worker.

8. Then she interviewed someone who made her fairly hopeful.

9. Jorge was quite smart.

10. He also dressed rather neatly.

Lesson 9

Put the verbs in the correct form of the present tense.

1. Ronnie (wake) up at 7 A.M.

2. She (dress) quickly.

3. Ronnie (eat) her breakfast.

4. She (grab) her purse.

5. She (wait) for the bus.

6. Ronnie (meet) Ed on the bus.

7. They (talk) about their work.

8. They (say) good-bye.

9. Ronnie (run) to catch another bus.

10. Ed (walk) to his office.

Lesson 10

Put the verbs in the correct form of the present continuous tense.

1. Many people (go) to the concert.

2. They (buy) their tickets.

3. Some (wait) in line.

4. My friends (walk) to their seats.

5. They (hope) that the concert starts on time.

6. Everyone (wait) patiently.

7. People (sing).

8. Some (play) tapes and CDs.

9. At last, the group (walk) on the stage.

10. Now everyone (clap).

Lesson 11

Put the verbs in the correct form of the past tense.

1. Chantelle (move) from South Carolina.

2. She (want) to live in New York.

3. Her brother (ask) her to stay with him.

4. Chantelle (want) to live in an apartment with her friend.

5. They (look) for an apartment for 2 weeks.

6. Finally, they (find) one.

7. They (move) their belongings in on September 1.

8. They (shop) for furniture.

9. Chantelle (buy) a new sofa.

10. Juanita (want) a desk.

Lesson 12

Put the verbs in the correct form of the future tense.

1. My parents (arrive) next week.

2. They (stay) with us for 3 weeks.

3. We (take) them to a play.

4. They (see) the new museum.

5. We (visit) our cousins.

6. On Friday, my mother and I (shop) for clothing.

7. My father and sister (have) a picnic in the park.

8. We (meet) for dinner at a seafood restaurant.

9. On Saturday, everyone (attend) Junior's graduation.

10. We (take) lots of pictures.

Answers for Unit 1 Review begin on page 120.

Unit 2 Review
Lesson 13

Add words of your own to each group of words below to make it a sentence. Make sure that the sentence begins with a capital letter and ends with a period. Write your sentences on the answer blanks.

1. hopes to become a teacher _____

2. she wants to _____

3. everybody thinks she _____

4. I hope _____

5. next year _____

Lesson 14

Each sentence below does one of the following: *makes a statement, asks a question, makes a request or gives a command,* or *shows strong feeling.* On the answer blank next to each sentence, write what each sentence does.

1. Will you come to the movies with me? _____

2. The movie begins at 3 P.M. _____

3. Bring your brother. _____

4. Be on time! _____

5. The movie is going to be crowded. _____

6. Could you take me home when it's over? _____

7. We can have dinner at my house. _____

8. What do you like to eat? _____

9. I love chili! _____

10. Please bring some dessert. _____

Lesson 15

Underline the subject in each sentence.

1. Jenna is an actress.

2. She is playing the part of a queen.

3. The audience loves her.

4. She performs every evening except Sunday.

5. Jenna loves her work.

6. Learning her lines is easy.

7. She reads them over and over.

8. Her mother helps her, too.

9. Her family has seen the play 12 times!

10. They love it.

Lesson 16

Three of the pairs of subjects and verbs below are sentences.
Underline the sentences.

1. Phillip wants.

2. The dog waits.

3. I am sitting.

4. Keith covers.

5. Maryanne puts.

6. Edgar bought.

7. Marcus fills.

8. The day seems.

9. I sing.

10. You found.

Lesson 17

Underline the thought completer in each sentence.

1. Fish breathe water.

2. Termites build huge nests.

3. A cheetah is a big cat that comes from Africa.

4. Cheetahs run as fast as 70 miles per hour.

5. Whales breathe air.

6. Monkeys spend a lot of time in trees.

7. Elephants eat leaves from trees.

8. Moles live in underground tunnels.

9. Spiders use two different kinds of thread to make their webs.

10. A mother dog carries her puppies in her mouth.

Lesson 18

Five of the subjects and verbs below agree. Five do not. Write Correct on the answer blank after the subjects and verbs that agree. If the subjects and verbs do not agree, write the verb on the answer blank that makes the subject and verb agree.

1. Donna place her books on the table. _____

2. William hangs up his coat. _____

3. Mary leaves her shoes by the bed. _____

4. Angelo look for his keys. _____

5. Claudia and Joe talks on the phone. _____

6. The dogs bark at the mail carrier. _____

7. A visitor enter the house. _____

8. Two people watch TV. _____

9. Mark cooks in the kitchen. _____

10. Bob and Tara waits for their son to come home. _____

Lesson 19

Underline the correct pronouns.

1. (He, Him) invited (her, she) to dinner.

2. (We, Us) gave (her, she) some tickets.

3. Our teacher told (him, he) and (me, I) to listen.

4. Joshua saw (us, we) at the park.

5. Did you leave it for (I, me)?

Lesson 20

Underline the thought completer in each sentence. On the answer blank, write S if the connector links the subjects, TC if the connector links the thought completers, or V if the connector links the verbs.

1. Tina and Tony went to the beach on Saturday. _____

2. They took a train and a bus. _____

3. At the beach, they swam and sunbathed. _____

4. Tony brought drinks and sandwiches. _____

5. Tina was supposed to bring a sheet or a blanket. _____

Lesson 21

Each item below contains two simple sentences. Read these sentences. Then combine them into one sentence using a comma and a connector. Write the compound sentence on the answer blank.

1. The weather is terrible. We will play the football game anyway.

_____

2. There's no gas in Ida's car. She won't be able to pick you up.

_____

3. I called Vic this morning. He had already left for school.

_____

4. Alice can't come to the party. She said she would bring a present next week.

_____

5. Our team has never won a championship. This year doesn't look like an exception.

_____

Answers for Unit 2 Review begin on page 122.

Unit Reviews

Unit 3 Review
Lesson 22

One sentence in the paragraph below does not relate to the main idea. Read the sentences. Then, on the answer blank, write the sentence that does *not* relate to the main idea.

I have been studying very hard for the GED exam. The exam will be held next Saturday at Bryant School on North Main Street. On North Main Street, there are many great places to eat. The test begins at 9 A.M. I hope I do well. I think I will!

_____

Lesson 23

Read the paragraph below. Decide which sentence is the topic sentence. Underline the topic sentence.

There are many different kinds of storms. Tornadoes are the most violent. Hurricanes can bring strong winds and rain. Thunder and lightning storms can cause great damage and loss of lives.

Lesson 24

The following paragraph is arranged in one of these ways: time order, spatial order, or order of importance. Read the paragraph. Then, on the answer blank, write the order in which the details are arranged.

I would like to work as the assistant manager in a restaurant this summer. Working as a manager will give me the money I need to attend school in the fall. I would like to manage my own restaurant one day. Working as an assistant manager will give me valuable experience. Also, I think it will be a lot of fun!

_____

Lesson 25

Here are the names of four characters. Choose one. Underline the one you choose. Write five details about what this character might look like, act like, or wear.

Happy Hannah   Sly Susie

Sad Sydney   Shy Sam

1. _____   4. _____

2. _____   5. _____

3. _____

Here are four settings in which a story could take place. Choose one setting. Underline the one you choose. Write five details about how the place looks. Include sounds, smells, and sights.

a sports stadium   a crowded elevator

a field of flowers   an amusement park

6. _____   9. _____

7. _____   10. _____

8. _____

Write five events that could take place in a story that has the character and setting you chose from above.

11. _____

12. _____

13. _____

14. _____

15. _____

Lesson 26

Read these sentences about making scrambled eggs. Then number the sentences in the order in which they should appear.

_____ Serve the eggs.

_____ Beat the eggs.

_____ Stir the eggs in the pan until they are cooked.

_____ Take the pan off the burner.

_____ Crack the eggs into a bowl.

_____ Pour the eggs into a pan.

Lesson 27

Here is one person's opinion about why the legal driving age should be raised. Underline the sentence that you feel does *not* belong in a paragraph expressing an opinion on this subject.

The legal driving age should be raised in our state. Most accidents are caused by younger drivers. They think they will live forever, so they don't drive carefully. Many younger kids drink while they drive, too. I like soda better than juice, and I hate beer. Our roads would be a lot safer if the driving age were raised.

Lesson 28

Here are three possible topic sentences. Underline the one that you think would be best in a paragraph about Abraham Lincoln.

Abraham Lincoln was very tall and had a beard.

Abraham Lincoln, the sixteenth President of the United States, is one of the most famous presidents in history.

Abraham Lincoln was killed on April 14, 1865.

Lesson 29

The paragraph below has one mistake in subject–verb agreement, one example of a verb that is not in the correct tense, and one group of words that is not a sentence. Read the paragraph. Then, rewrite it carefully on the answer blanks. Correct all the errors.

Today is the last day of school. Rosemary want to celebrate. She and Harry plan to go out for a special dinner. a new restaurant. They loved trying new kinds of food.

_____

_____

_____

_____

_____

Answers for Unit 3 Review begin on page 123.

Answers

LESSON 1

Practice

Answers will vary. Here are some hints:

1. Insert the name of a person.
2. Insert the name of a thing (such as a cookie or a vacation).
3. Insert the name of a person and an action (for example, Janet works).
4. Insert the name of a place (for example, office, station, or house).
5. Insert a kind of action (for example, drive or work).
6. Insert the name of a man.
7. Insert the name of a person and an action (for example, Hector sleeps).
8. Insert an action (rings, falls).
9. Insert a person's name in the first answer blank and the name of a thing in the second blank (for example, Dinell, TV).
10. Insert the name of a person and an action (for example, Mike sings).

LESSON 2

Practice

1. Clyde, waiter, restaurant
2. George, cook
3. restaurant, George, hamburger
4. Clyde, steak, potato
5. day, George, dessert
6. Ethel, Julia, pie
7. Rodriguez, dessert
8. smile, face
9. Rodriguez, hand, cook
10. pie, item, menu

LESSON 3

Practice

1. cars
2. engines
3. pistons
4. rings
5. valves
6. cars, tires
7. treads, tires
8. Mufflers, problems.
9. brakes
10. radios

LESSON 4

Practice

1. me   **2.** She   **3.** you, their

4. his   **5.** your   **6.** They, her

7. him   **8.** us   **9.** our

10. its

LESSON 5

Practice

1. some   **2.** a, new   **3.** brick, dirt

4. three   **5.** The, three, two   **6.** a, beautiful, a, large

7. The, big   **8.** green, the, large, a yellow, the, small   **9.** brown, a, black

10. early

LESSON 6

Practice

1. threw   **2.** jumped   **3.** bounced   **4.** dribbled

5. moved   **6.** passed   **7.** caught   **8.** raced

9. leaped   **10.** slammed

LESSON 7

Practice

1. quickly   **2.** accurately   **3.** carefully   **4.** slowly

5. totally   **6.** fast   **7.** carelessly   **8.** recklessly

9. slowly   **10.** safely

LESSON 8

Practice

1. too   **2.** quite   **3.** really   **4.** truly

5. very   **6.** pretty   **7.** unusually   **8.** rather, quickly

9. extremely   **10.** very

LESSON 9

Practice

1. begins   **2.** walks   **3.** whisper   **4.** takes

5. walks   **6.** speaks   **7.** listens   **8.** moves

9. returns   **10.** sends

LESSON 10

Practice 1

1. are applying
2. are filling out
3. are hoping
4. is leaving
5. is looking

Practice 2

1. All the applicants look for work. *are looking*
2. Several work at other jobs. *are working*
3. One person asks to borrow a pen. *is asking*
4. Another person thinks about his family. *is thinking*
5. Everyone waits nervously for an interview. *is waiting*

LESSON 11

Practice

1. traveled
2. visited
3. shopped
4. toured
5. walked
6. liked
7. tasted
8. enjoyed
9. watched
10. admired

LESSON 12

Practice

1. will visit
2. will tour
3. will walk
4. will photograph
5. will see
6. will read
7. will buy
8. will ride
9. will drive
10. will shine

LESSON 13

Practice

1. My friend Willie is a bus driver.
2. He goes to work at 7 A.M. every weekday.
3. Answers will vary. One possible answer is: Willie does not work on weekends.
4. Answers will vary. One possible answer is: He is driving an old bus.
5. He has never had an accident.
6. One possible answer is: Willie always tries hard to be nice to the people who ride the bus.
7. He was voted the most helpful bus driver.
8. Answers may vary. One possible answer is: He keeps the award on the dashboard.

LESSON 14

Practice

1. My apartment is not in good condition. *Makes a statement*
2. Have you seen the walls? *Asks a question*
3. Come and take a look. *Gives a command*
4. This is terrible! *Shows strong feeling*
5. I've called the landlord three times. *Makes a statement*
6. He is always too busy to answer the phone. *Makes a statement*
7. Everything is leaking! *Shows strong feeling*
8. I can't stand it another minute! *Shows strong feeling*
9. Do you think I can sue him? *Asks a question*
10. Please help me right away! *Makes a request*

LESSON 15

Practice 1

1. Ida
2. muscles
3. Paul
4. Swimming
5. Henry
6. Maria
7. Jogging
8. I
9. Serving
10. Exercising

Practice 2

Answers will vary.

LESSON 16

Practice

1. They are walking.
2. Nina dropped. (You don't know what Nina dropped.)
3. I like. (You don't know what the person, "I," likes.)
4. The suit looked. (You don't know what the suit looked like.)
5. Al sneezed.
6. Marva will work.
7. Luis sounds. (You don't know what Luis sounds like.)
8. We are taking. (You don't know what these people, "we," are taking.)
9. The cat wants. (You don't know what the cat wants.)
10. The dog is sleeping.

LESSON 17

Practice

1. her relatives   2. in Maine   3. by bus

4. 18 hours   5. to ride on buses   6. an entire book

7. at the sights   8. her eyes to rest   9. a snack of crackers

10. the trip

LESSON 18

Practice

1. Uri want a new TV. *wants*
2. Daisy likes to travel. *Correct*
3. The students and teachers reads out loud. *read*
4. The plumber fix the sink. *fixes*
5. Beatrice call her mother every week. *calls*
6. The singers and actors hope for success. *Correct*
7. The cats leap onto the sofa. *Correct*
8. A swimmer dive into the pool. *dives*
9. Her shoes squeak. *Correct*
10. Radios and stereos plays too loud. *play*

LESSON 19

Practice

1. I   2. She   3. she   4. her

5. me   6. me   7. She, them   8. They

9. her, us   10. We

LESSON 20

Practice

1. Rita and Tomas are getting married this summer. *S*
2. The wedding will be in a church or a large hall. *TC*
3. They are inviting friends and relatives. *TC*
4. Rita's sister designs and makes clothes. *V*
5. She will make the bridal gown and the bridesmaids' dresses. *TC*
6. The bridesmaids are Wendy, Tanya, and Cara. *TC*
7. Rita's brother or Tomas's friend will be the best man. *S*
8. There will be lots of singing and dancing at the wedding. *TC*

LESSON 21

Practice

1. Jeanette works in a bookstore on weekdays, and she works in a restaurant on weekends. (*And* is the connector because the two thoughts are closely related. They both tell things that Jeanette does.)
2. She is very busy, so she doesn't have much time to see her friends. (*So* is the connector because one thing happens because of the other.)
3. Jeanette likes to read about life in other countries, but her mother likes to read about history. (*But* is the connector because it shows a contrast between what Jeanette likes and what her mother likes.)
4. Her friend Denzel likes mystery books, so she looks for mysteries when a new shipment of books arrives. (*So* is the connector because one thing happens because of the other.)
5. Jeanette would like to be the store manager, or she would like to travel. (*Or* is the connector because it shows a choice.)

LESSON 22

Practice

1. I have a horrible cold today.
2. My mother lives in Florida.
3. Sharks are always a danger in the waters.

None of these sentences relates to the main idea. The main idea is that being a travel agent isn't easy, which is stated in the first sentence.

LESSON 23

Practice

1. The topic sentence is: Working at a refreshment stand is my summer job. All the other sentences in the paragraph give information about working at a refreshment stand.
2. The topic sentence is: Mickey Mouse is probably the most famous cartoon character in the world. All the other sentences in the paragraph are about Mickey Mouse.
3. The topic sentence is *High Noon* is considered one of the best films about the West. All the other sentences in the paragraph are about *High Noon*.

LESSON 24

Practice

1. Order of importance. The most important thing to see is mentioned first. The next most important places are mentioned second. The least important things are mentioned last.
2. Time order. Things are mentioned in the order in which they happened.
3. Spatial order. Every sentence locates Washington, D.C., on a map in relation to other places.

LESSON 25

Practice 1

1. We lay in the sun until we were very hot.
2. After we were hot enough, we raced into the water.
3. We dried off and ate a delicious picnic lunch.

Practice 2

Answers will vary.

Practice 3

Answers will vary.

LESSON 26

Practice

Get special nail clippers from a pet store. Hold the cat on your lap or put the cat on a table in front of you. Lift one of the front legs. Hold the cat's toe with your thumb and forefinger. Your finger should be on the bottom of the toe, and your thumb should be on the top. When you press your finger and thumb together, the claw will move outward. Clip the tip of the claw just where it begins to curve downward. Be sure not to clip the pink area of the claw, because this will cause bleeding. Clip all the claws on one paw. Then do the same thing to the claws on the other paw.

LESSON 27

Practice

The two sentences that do not belong in the paragraph are: Most kids hate school, but who cares? and In some countries, kids don't even go to school at all, so look how lucky we are.

LESSON 28

Practice 1

The best topic sentence would be: In many zoos today, animals roam freely over large land areas that have trees and grass and other wildlife.

Practice 2

1. Order of importance   **2.** Spatial order   **3.** Time order

LESSON 29

Practice

Jed is my best friend. He is moving to Florida. Jed wants to move. He loves warm weather. He likes to water ski. He and his brother love to swim. Jed enjoys playing tennis. I will miss him.

Unit 1 Review

LESSON 1

Answers will vary. Some possible answers are:

1. Thanksgiving
2. same school
3. boring
4. My father
5. I love to read
6. Henry, the store to buy eggs
7. wagged its tail when it saw me
8. is the best season of the year
9. an apartment near my house
10. attend college next year

LESSON 2

1. squirrel
2. bird
3. cat
4. creature, earth
5. turtle, shell
6. whale, animal, world
7. wolf, person
8. cow, grass, hay
9. spider, web
10. mouse, wall

LESSON 3

1. birds, nests, twigs
2. Camels, humps
3. sharks
4. insects
5. bones
6. Lions, zebras
7. Bees
8. dogs, wolves
9. Clams, shells
10. Snakes, elephants

LESSON 4

1. I, her
2. She, me
3. We, him
4. us
5. We, our
6. He, them
7. him
8. They, us, her
9. We, our, you
10. It, her

LESSON 5

1. a, red
2. The, new, leather
3. Five, the
4. two, a, long
5. the, large, the
6. the, old
7. the, new
8. the, next
9. the, football
10. The, a, great

LESSON 6

1. bought
2. carried
3. chopped
4. peeled
5. boiled
6. washed
7. cut
8. placed
9. put
10. served

LESSON 7

1. slowly	**2.** gracefully	**3.** fast	**4.** quickly
5. gladly	**6.** carefully	**7.** beautifully	**8.** proudly
9. often	**10.** never		

LESSON 8

1. very, carefully	**2.** more, quickly	**3.** fairly
4. almost	**5.** fast, so, fast	**6.** really, fast, extremely, accurately
7. never	**8.** fairly	**9.** quite
10. rather, neatly		

LESSON 9

Underline the present tense verb in each sentence.

1. wakes up	**2.** dresses	**3.** eats	**4.** grabs
5. waits	**6.** meets	**7.** talk	**8.** say
9. runs	**10.** walks		

LESSON 10

1. are going	**2.** are buying	**3.** are waiting	**4.** are walking
5. are hoping	**6.** is waiting	**7.** are singing	**8.** are playing
9. is walking	**10.** is clapping		

LESSON 11

1. moved	**2.** wanted	**3.** asked	**4.** wanted
5. looked	**6.** found	**7.** moved	**8.** shopped
9. bought	**10.** wanted		

LESSON 12

1. will arrive	**2.** will stay	**3.** will take	**4.** will see
5. will visit	**6.** will shop	**7.** will have	**8.** will meet
9. will attend	**10.** will take		

Unit 2 Review

Answers will vary. Some possible answers are:

1. Carla hopes to become a teacher.
2. She wants to get married in the spring.
3. Everybody thinks she will make a beautiful bride.
4. I hope she teaches in my daughter's school.
5. Next year my son will be in kindergarten.

LESSON 14

1. Asks a question	2. Makes a statement	3. Makes a request
4. Gives a command	5. Makes a statement	6. Asks a question
7. Makes a statement	8. Asks a question	9. Shows strong feeling
10. Makes a request		

LESSON 15

1. Jenna	2. She	3. The audience	4. She
5. Jenna	6. Learning	7. She	8. Her mother
9. Her family	10. They		

LESSON 16

Only the following three pairs of subjects and verbs are sentences: **2, 3, 9**. All the other pairs of subjects and verbs need thought completers; they do not express complete thoughts.

LESSON 17

1. water
2. huge nests
3. a big cat that comes from Africa
4. as fast as 70 miles per hour
5. air
6. a lot of time in trees
7. leaves from trees
8. in underground tunnels
9. two different kinds of thread to make their webs
10. her puppies in her mouth

LESSON 18

1. Donna place her books on the table. *places*
2. William hangs up his coat. *Correct*
3. Mary leaves her shoes by the bed. *Correct*
4. Angelo look for his keys. *looks*
5. Claudia and Joe talks on the phone. *talk*

6. The dogs bark at the mail carrier. *Correct*
7. A visitor enter the house. *enters*
8. Two people watch TV. *Correct*
9. Mark cooks in the kitchen. *Correct*
10. Bob and Tara waits for their son to come home. *wait*

LESSON 19

1. He, her
2. We, her
3. him, me
4. us
5. me

LESSON 20

1. Tina and Tony went to the beach on Saturday. *S*
2. They took a train and a bus. *TC*
3. At the beach, they swam and sunbathed. *V*
4. Tony brought drinks and sandwiches. *TC*
5. Tina was supposed to bring a sheet or a blanket. *TC*

LESSON 21

Possible answers are:

1. The weather is terrible, but we will play the football game anyway.
2. There's no gas in Ida's car, so she won't be able to pick you up.
3. I called Vic this morning, but he had already left for school.
4. Alice can't come to the party, but she said she would bring a present next week.
5. Our team has never won a championship, and this year doesn't look like an exception.

Unit 3 Review

LESSON 22

The sentence that does not relate to the main idea is: On North Main Street, there are many great places to eat.

LESSON 23

The topic sentence is: There are many different kinds of storms.

LESSON 24

order of importance

LESSON 25

Answers will vary. Here are examples for the character, Shy Sam (items 1–5), in the setting, an amusement park (items 6–10), with 5 events (items 11–15).

1. Shy Sam is very tall and thin.
2. He wears jeans and a green T-shirt.
3. He likes to play computer games by himself.
4. When a girl talks to him, he usually does not look at her.
5. He goes out only when he is lonely.
6. When he comes to the amusement park, it is very crowded.
7. The sun is hot and there is a lot of loud music.
8. Sam smells popcorn, hotdogs, and hamburgers.
9. Men shout for people to come see the sideshows and play games.
10. People on fast "rides" scream and laugh.
11. Sam walks into a field to get away from the noise.
12. Some boys see him and chase him.
13. Sam runs away and goes into a sideshow.
14. He sits down next to a girl, and she smiles at him.
15. They talk, and Sam walks her home.

LESSON 26

6 Serve the eggs.
2 Beat the eggs.
4 Stir the eggs in the pan until they are cooked.
5 Take the pan off the burner.
1 Crack the eggs into a bowl.
3 Pour the eggs into a pan.

LESSON 27

The sentence that does not belong is: I like soda better than juice, and I hate beer.

LESSON 28

The best topic sentence would be: Abraham Lincoln, the sixteenth President of the United States, is one of the most famous presidents in history.

LESSON 29

Today is the last day of school. Rosemary wants to celebrate. She and Harry plan to go out for a special dinner. They will go to a new restaurant. They love trying new kinds of food.